ROBERT'S RULES
OF ORDER
NEWLY REVISED
In Brief

ROBERT'S RULES OF ORDER
NEWLY REVISED
In Brief

UPDATED TO ACCORD WITH
THE ELEVENTH EDITION
OF THE COMPLETE MANUAL

HENRY M. ROBERT III
WILLIAM J. EVANS
DANIEL H. HONEMANN
THOMAS J. BALCH

with the assistance of
DANIEL E. SEABOLD
SHMUEL GERBER

Da Capo Press

Text design by Lisa Kreinbrink
Set in 10-point Goudy by Eclipse Publishing Services

Robert's rules of order newly revised in brief—2nd ed.
ISBN 978-0-306-82019-9
Cataloging-in-Publication Data is available from the Library of Congress
Library of Congress Control Number: 2011932261

For questions and answers and further information on parliamentary
procedure visit www.robertsrules.com

Published by Da Capo Press
an imprint of Perseus Books, LLC,
a subsidiary of Hachette Book Group, Inc.
www.dacapopress.com

Da Capo Press books are available at special discounts for bulk purchases in
the U.S. by corporations, institutions, and other organizations. For more
information, please contact the Special Markets Department at Perseus
Books, 2300 Chestnut Street, Suite 200, Philadelphia, PA 19103, or call
(800) 810-4145, ext. 5000, or e-mail special.markets@perseusbooks.com.

20 19 18 17 16 15 14 13 12

In a land where perhaps most persons . . .
are members of one or more societies,
some knowledge of parliamentary [procedure]
may be justly regarded as a necessary part
of the education of every man and woman. . . .

—HENRY M. ROBERT

CONTENTS

ROBERT'S RULES OF ORDER
NEWLY REVISED
In Brief

Part I

WHY HAVE RULES?

THE "WHY AND WHEREFORE" OF MEETING RULES

How many times have you been to a meeting that didn't go well? Did it seem that the chair didn't keep order? Was there a feeling that something was "railroaded"? Did it take an interminable amount of time to settle the simplest things? What was wrong?

When people want to do something as a group, they must first agree on exactly what it is they want to do and how they want to go about it. In other words, they must work together to make some decisions. Sometimes it may take some zeroing in even to get at the "what?" At other times that may be generally understood and the necessary decisions may involve mostly the "how to?"

If there are only three or four persons in the group, you are right if you wonder why they should need a book like this. Common sense tells us that all they need to do is sit down in one room as people bent on working out where they want to go in a courteous spirit without wasting anyone's time. They should all try to agree; but if they can't and a majority want to go ahead with something, the group may want to have an understanding that the majority's will should prevail. Whoever is taking the lead may want to note down what has been decided and provide each person with a copy.

But make it even a half dozen people who are meeting in this way, and you will soon see the need for at least some formal control.

Too many people may try to talk at once. Some may not be able to get a word in edgewise. People may wander off the subject—or may even lose sight of what the proper subject is. And if things aren't handled right, they may come out of the meeting with different understandings of what was or was not agreed to.

To prevent this, you will need to pick one person to "chair" the meeting—to designate who may speak at any given time and to see that the discussion narrows down to specific, precisely worded proposals. These should be recorded, and should be voted on unless there is obvious total agreement.

When the gathering reaches a size of about 12 to 15 persons, another threshold is crossed. At that point, the meeting becomes essentially "full scale," with a need for tighter, more formal, more carefully developed control. A certain paradox appears. In order to preserve its freedom to act, the body must impose regulation.

The needed control must not only "keep order." It must of course be geared to getting the business done and resolving any issues that may arise along the way. But—even more important—it must do these things in a way that's *fair* to everyone taking part in the process. And in this there's more than may meet the eye.

Control of this kind naturally must be imposed by the person who conducts the meeting—generally called the chairman. There are a multitude of details that must be determined through him or her. Who gets to speak when? How is the meeting to be kept on track? What if discussion tends to go on forever? How is intense disagreement to be handled? How can business best be put through when there is no disagreement? What if a proposal appears to be not yet in shape for a yes-or-no decision? And in a group like a club that has a continuing existence, how is business to be carried over from one meeting to the next if that seems desirable? All these things and many more are potential stumbling blocks when a large number of people are involved.

Whoever is chairman will soon come up against a significant fact of life related to gatherings of this kind. In them, *it is virtually impos-*

sible for any human being to perform the function of chairman fairly under all the situations that may arise, without a considerable body of established rules to go by. No one can do it just out of his or her own head.

Parliamentary procedure is the name given to the tradition of rules and customs that has grown up in the civilized world for dealing with these problems. A bit of it goes back as far as the ancient Greeks. But its basic content was mainly formed by centuries of trial and error in the English Parliament, from which the name *"parliamentary* procedure" comes.

Not everyone may realize that the organizations most of us get involved in at some time or other are essentially similar to great legislative assemblies in an important way. They all meet to *decide on actions to be taken.* For this reason, they are all known as **deliberative assemblies**.

Major law-making bodies usually develop their own particular rules. This is largely impractical, however, in ordinary organizations as far as rules of meeting procedure are concerned. Each group of this kind obviously must work out its own structure. But things work best if most of the rules for making decisions in meetings are the same from group to group. Obviously, it would be worse than burdensome if one had to use different rules for deciding matters every time he or she took part in a different organization. By general understanding in our culture, parliamentary procedure fills the role of supplying this needed common body of rules.

Although originally derived from practices in the English Parliament, parliamentary procedure as it exists in America today has gradually evolved somewhat differently. Henry Martyn Robert (1837–1923), a distinguished engineer who retired from the U.S. Army as a brigadier general, had considerable influence on this development. A self-taught, in-depth student of the subject who was active in many organizations, he first published his *Robert's Rules of Order* while a major in 1876. It rapidly became accepted as the standard authoritative work on meeting rules—so much so that when people talk about using correct procedure in a meeting, they often speak of doing it "according to Robert's Rules."

As Henry Robert first conceived his book, he wanted it to be brief and simple enough to serve as a guide in the hands of every meeting-goer. He thought it might run to about 50 pages. By the time the first edition was published, he found he needed 176. Following its publication, letters asking questions about parliamentary situations not clearly answered in the book began to pour in—by the hundreds through the years.

Consequently, over time, he was obliged to add more and more pages to answer the most common of these questions. Robert himself repeatedly revised his 1876 book. In accordance with his expressed wishes, his son, his widow, and his daughter-in-law all carried on the work after his death. And now his grandson, Henry M. Robert III, is among the team of parliamentarians (as experts in these rules are called in this country) chosen by his descendants to continue the updating and revision of the book. The manual is now in its eleventh edition under the title of *Robert's Rules of Order Newly Revised*—commonly abbreviated RONR.*

RONR, the complete rule book, now contains 669 pages of text, plus tables and index. All of its content has to be there because it *may* be needed, and has at some time come up as a question of procedure somewhere. RONR is designed as a reference book providing, as nearly as possible, an answer to any question of parliamentary procedure that may be met with.

But the average person doesn't have to know all this to be able to function effectively in most ordinary meetings, or even to chair one. At least 80 percent of the content of RONR will be needed less than 20 percent of the time.

---

*This is the standard abbreviation parliamentarians use to cite Henry M. Robert III and others, *Robert's Rules of Order Newly Revised*, 11th ed. (Cambridge, Mass.: Da Capo Press, 2011). The standard citation to particular pages and lines is "RONR (11th ed. [for 'edition']), p. or pp. [for 'page' or 'pages'], l. or ll. [for 'line' or 'lines']."

For one who will brave it, RONR is written to serve as a self-explanatory text that can be read through, with topics presented in an order that will best convey an overall understanding of the entire subject matter. You need not apologize, however, if you find that to be a bigger project than you would like to take on at this point.

If you are such a person, and want to know how to get by in a meeting or as a club president, this brief book is for you.

The commonly needed basics of parliamentary procedure are well within the grasp of any person of ordinary schooling. By reading this book, you can learn them easily, step by step. For those to whom parliamentary procedure has seemed something of a mystery, this book should quickly bring that to an end.

It is important to understand, though, that this introductory book is *not* itself the rule book. Only the complete *Robert's Rules of Order Newly Revised*—RONR—is that. To keep to the framework of a simple guide, this book omits a great many rules, avoids certain subject areas altogether, and doesn't get into many exceptions to the rules it does include. It is the rules in RONR that govern, and nothing in this book may be cited instead of or in conflict with RONR. To help ready reference to the complete rules, each subject covered here is cross-referenced to the pages of its fuller treatment in RONR. By reading this book you will learn how to find the additional rules in RONR if you need them.

Because this book is only an introduction and guide to RONR, it is not itself suitable for adoption by any organization as its **"parliamentary authority"**—the book of rules the group names to govern its meeting procedure. If any organization designates this book as its parliamentary authority, it actually adopts the current edition of *Robert's Rules of Order Newly Revised*.

A prime value of parliamentary procedure is that it provides processes through which an organization, large or small, can work out satisfactory solutions to the greatest number of questions in the least amount of time. It can do this whatever detail or complexity may be involved. It makes meetings go smoothly when everyone is in agreement, and allows the group to come to decisions fairly when issues are bitterly contested.

A chairman should never be stricter than is necessary for the good of the meeting. But, within that pattern, parliamentary procedure should normally be followed as a matter of course if it is to work well. It's not something to look to only when you get into trouble.

Robert's Rules of Order has brought order to millions of meetings. Yet it has more to offer us if the core of its content can penetrate more deeply into our culture. Every parliamentarian has heard many stories of meeting participants finding themselves helpless in the face of badly, ineptly—even unfairly—run meetings. All this need not be! Effective meetings could become the universal rule, if an elementary knowledge of the accepted rules that govern them were to become the common property of most people, as—for example—are the rules of baseball. The authors hope this brief book will play some part in bringing about that result.

Now let's start at the beginning, with what happens in a meeting.

Part II

SO YOU'RE GOING TO A MEETING

WHAT HAPPENS AT A MEETING?

CHAPTER CONTENTS

A. THE ROLES OF THE PRESIDING OFFICER AND THE SECRETARY

To keep order, one person is chosen to **preside** over the meeting. This person enforces the rules and designates who is to speak at any given time. The presiding officer may be elected specifically for the meeting, and is then called the **chairman**.* More commonly, he or she is elected to serve for a term of a year or more, with a title such as **president**. While actually presiding, the presiding officer is called **"the chair."**

To make a written record of what is done, usually called the **minutes**, a **secretary** is elected.**

B. QUORUM

In most organizations that have regular meetings, many members are often absent. The organization should not be bound by decisions taken by an unrepresentatively small number of members who might attend a meeting. To prevent this, a **quorum**—a minimum number of members who must be present—is required for a meeting to conduct substantive business.

Organizations usually decide what should be the quorum required for their meetings.† If an organization fails to do this, then—with some exceptions—the quorum is a majority of the members. ("Majority" means more than half.††)

---

*"Chairman" is the long-established usage. Several variations—such as "chairperson" or "chair"—are now frequently used.

**The presiding officer and the secretary are the minimum essential officers. RONR (11th ed.), p. 22, ll. 1–23. Minutes are explained in Chapter 16 of this book and more fully in RONR (11th ed.), pages 468–76.

†An organization specifies its quorum in its *bylaws*, which are explained in Chapter 10.

††See also q. 4 on pp. 114–15.

When no quorum is present the meeting can do only a very limited number of things, such as set the time and place for another meeting. Any substantive action taken in the absence of a quorum is invalid.* Even when a meeting begins with a quorum present, it loses its right to conduct substantive business whenever enough members leave to bring attendance below the level of a quorum. It can resume substantive business only when enough members return, or other members arrive, to give it a quorum again.

C. A STANDARD ORDER OF BUSINESS

A meeting begins when it is **called to order** by the presiding officer. The chairman or president takes his or her place and says in a clear voice, **"The meeting will come to order."** There may then be opening ceremonies, such as saying the Pledge of Allegiance. Most meetings follow a traditional **order of business**. Simplified,** this includes:

Simplified Standard Order of Business

Reading and Approval of Minutes
Reports
Unfinished Business
New Business

---

*RONR (11th ed.), pp. 345–49. See, however, RONR (11th ed.), pages 124–25 for the ratification of action taken without a quorum.

**In fact, the "standard" order of business is a little more complicated. For full details, see RONR (11th ed.), pages 26, 353–63. Organizations may prefer to adopt their own order of business, adapted to the specific needs of the group. RONR (11th ed.), p. 16, ll. 2–8.

1. Reading and Approval of Minutes

The chair says, **"The Secretary will read the minutes."** When the secretary has read them, the chair says, **"Are there any corrections to the minutes?"** Normally, corrections are made without objection, but if there is a dispute there can be debate and a vote on the proposed correction. Thereafter, the chair says, **"If there are no [further] corrections, the minutes are approved."**

Only after the minutes of a meeting are approved in this way do they become the official record of what happened. Often, the secretary sends out draft minutes of the previous meeting before the meeting at which they are to be approved. If this happens, they don't have to be actually read at the meeting unless a member insists. When draft minutes have been sent to the members, the chair might begin by saying, **"The minutes of the previous meeting have been distributed. Are there any corrections to the minutes?"** [RONR (11th ed.), pp. 354–55.]

2. Reports

The assembly then hears reports from officers, boards, and committees of the organization. (More about boards and committees in Chapters 6, 18, and 19.) The chair might say, for example: **"May we have the Treasurer's report?" "The chair recognizes the chairman of the Membership Committee for a report." "Does the Program Committee have a report?"**

Often, these reports just give information. Sometimes, however, they include recommendations for action by the assembly. These recommendations are then considered by the group—debated and voted on—at the end of the report containing them. [RONR (11th ed.), pp. 355–56.]

3. Unfinished Business

Following reports, the group moves on to consider items of business, if any, carried over from the previous meeting. The chair should bring these matters up automatically, normally beginning with any unfinished item that was in the middle of being considered when the previous meeting adjourned. For example, the chair might say, **"Under unfinished business, the first item of business is the motion*** relating to . . . , which was pending when the last meeting adjourned. The question is on the adoption of the motion [stating the motion]. . . . [After this item has been disposed of:] **The next item of business is . . . ."**

In a properly conducted meeting, there is no type or class of business called "old business." It is a common mistake for the chair to call for "old business" and under that incorrect category to allow members to bring up again matters that were considered at earlier meetings or matters for which there was merely an informal suggestion that they should be brought up at the present meeting. In fact, what properly come up under the correct category, "unfinished business," are:

1) the item (if any) that was actually in the process of being considered when the last meeting adjourned, followed by
2) any items that were scheduled to come up at the last meeting but were not reached before its adjournment, in the order these were due to come up at that meeting. [RONR (11th ed.), p. 358, ll. 19–30. *See also footnote on page 53 of this book.*]

4. New Business

The chair asks, **"Is there any new business?"** New items may then be brought up by any member, using the procedure—making a motion—described in the next chapter. [RONR (11th ed.), p. 360.]

---

*"Motions" are explained in the next chapter.

D. AGENDA: AN ALTERNATIVE TO FOLLOWING A STANDARD ORDER OF BUSINESS

Instead of following a standard order of business, a group may adopt an **agenda**. An agenda sets out the order in which specific items are to be considered, and sometimes sets exact times for their consideration. Frequently, the president presents a draft agenda, but to be binding it must be adopted by the group at or soon after the start of the session.* The group may make any changes it wishes before voting to adopt it. [RONR (11th ed.), pp. 371–75; see also q. 14 on p. 120 of this book.]

Example of an Agenda

I. Opening Ceremonies		9:00 A.M.
	A. Invocation	Juan Hernandez, Chaplain
	B. Pledge of Allegiance	Led by Jane Simpson
II. Adoption of Agenda		
III. Reading and Approval of Minutes		
IV. Reports of Officers		
	A. President Sean Donahue	
	B. Vice-President Ahmed Hassan	
	C. Secretary Ben Choate	
	D. Treasurer Sandra Norris	
V. Report of Board of Directors	Secretary Ben Choate	
VI. Reports of Committees		
	A. Membership Committee	Mary Ng, Chairman
	B. Education Committee	Kim Dix, Chairman

(*continued on next page*)

---

*If the session is not already controlled by an order of business, then a majority vote is sufficient to adopt an agenda. In other circumstances, a greater vote may be required. See RONR (11th ed.), p. 372, ll. 11–22.

Example of an Agenda *(continued)*

VII. Recess for Lunch	12:30 P.M.
VIII. Reconvene	2:00 P.M.
IX. Program: Speaker Stephen Lang	2:05 P.M.
X. Consideration of Purchasing New Headquarters	
XI. New Business	
XII. Adjourn	

E. ADJOURNMENT, RECESS, AND STANDING AT EASE

When the meeting has completed its work, the chair says, **"Is there any further business? . . . Since there is no further business, the meeting is adjourned."** To **adjourn** means to close the meeting. Even if there is still business that has not been completed a majority may vote to adjourn.*

When the group wishes to take a short break from a meeting, it may vote (by a majority) to **recess**. The proposal to recess may set a time, as in, "recess for five minutes." Or it may be to "recess until called to order by the chair," which leaves it up to the presiding officer to decide when to end the recess and resume the meeting. [RONR (11th ed.), p. 82, ll. 15–25; pp. 230–33.]

The chair may cause a brief pause in the proceedings, if no member objects, by directing the group to **stand at ease**. This means that members remain in their places, perhaps talking quietly, until the chair again calls the meeting to order. [RONR (11th ed.), p. 82, ll. 26–33.]

---

*For other ways to adjourn, see RONR (11th ed.), pages 233–42.

CHAPTER

——

3

——

HOW DECISIONS ARE MADE AT A MEETING: HANDLING MOTIONS

CHAPTER CONTENTS

A. THE MEANING OF "MOTION"

The primary purpose of the sort of meeting that uses rules of order is for the group to make decisions. It may decide on anything from taking a position on a major public issue to organizing a pet show. To begin the process of making any decision, a member offers a proposal by *making a motion*. A **motion** is a formal proposal by a member, in a meeting, that the group take certain action. [RONR (11th ed.), p. 27, ll. 18–23.]

A **main motion** is one whose introduction brings business before an assembly. Strictly speaking, there should be no debate on a matter before a motion regarding it has been made. Only one main motion may be before the assembly for action at a time. [RONR (11th ed.), p. 34, l. 7 to p. 35, l. 2; p. 62, ll. 18–21; p. 100, ll. 3–5.]

B. HOW YOU GET TO SPEAK AT A MEETING

In order to make a motion or to speak in debate, you use the same procedure: You stand up immediately after the previous speaker has finished and call out "Madam President," "Mr. Chairman," or whatever the chair's title may be. The chair designates you as the next speaker, or **recognizes** you, normally by calling out your name or title, saying, for example, "Mr. Jackson," or "The delegate from Clayton County," or sometimes (in a small meeting) simply by nodding to you.

When you are authorized to speak in this way, you are said to **have the floor**. When finished, you sit down, and thus **yield the floor**. [RONR (11th ed.), pp. 29–31, 376–78.]

Getting Recognized to Speak

MEMBER A [Stands]: Madam President!

CHAIR: Mr. A.

MEMBER A: It's not a very good idea to . . . . [Sits when
finished speaking.]

C. HOW A MOTION GETS BEFORE
A GROUP

1. How to Make a Motion

To make a main motion, after obtaining the floor you simply say,
"I move that . . ." and then clearly describe the proposal. For example, **"I move that** the Tennis League establish a division open to
juniors and seniors enrolled in city high schools."

It is *very* important to say *precisely* what the words of the motion
are to be. The group votes on exact language, not on a vague idea. In
the end, each motion has to be written down in the minutes. It is the
secretary's job to copy the motions down accurately—not to come up
with language he or she thinks is what the group or the mover meant.

The chair can require that main motions be submitted by the
mover in writing. [RONR (11th ed.), p. 40, ll. 4–7.]

In fact, it is a good practice to write out any motion you propose
and make copies to give to both the president and the secretary. A
long or complex motion should *always* be written out and handed to
the secretary.

After making a motion, you immediately sit down. You wait until
later to give your reasons for making the proposal. [RONR (11th ed.),
pp. 33–35.]

Making a Motion

MEMBER A [Stands]: Madam President!

CHAIR: Mr. A.

MEMBER A: I move that the Tennis League establish a division open to juniors and seniors enrolled in city high schools. [When finished *making the motion*, be seated. Wait until later to explain why the motion is a good idea.]

2. "Seconding" a Motion

When one member has made a main motion, it must be **seconded** in order to be considered by the group. This shows that at least two members want the proposal considered; it does not necessarily mean the seconder agrees with the motion. If there is no second, the motion is not put before the group for discussion or decision.

To second a motion, you call out **"Second!"** You may remain seated, and you do *not* have to be recognized by the chair to second a motion. [RONR (11th ed.), pp. 35–37.]

3. The Chair "States" the Question

When a motion has been moved and seconded, the chair then **states the question** on the motion. To "state" a motion, the chair simply says, **"It is moved and seconded that"** and then repeats the exact words in which the motion was made. For example: **"It is moved and seconded that** the Tennis League establish a division open to juniors and seniors enrolled in city high schools."

The chair must state the question on a motion after it is moved and seconded for it to be properly before the group for consideration, for at least two reasons.

First, it is important that everyone in the group be able to know exactly what proposal is before it. By repeating the exact language of the motion, the chair helps everyone to hear it clearly, and calls everyone's attention to the fact that a new proposal is now ready to be considered.

Second, the chair has two duties, before stating any motion:

a) The chair must determine that the motion is in order at the time. If the motion in some way violates the rules, the chair does not state the motion, but instead says, **"The chair rules that the motion is not in order because . . . ."*** (The rules that govern when motions are in order will be described later.)

b) The chair must ensure that the motion is clearly phrased. If the motion is unclear, the chair should help the mover to reword it before stating it. [See pp. 136–37 of this book; RONR (11th ed.), pp. 37–42.]

Making, Seconding, and Stating a Motion

MEMBER A [Stands]: Madam President!

CHAIR: Mr. A.

MEMBER A: I move that the Tennis League establish a division open to juniors and seniors enrolled in city high schools. [When finished *making motion*, sit. Wait until later to explain why motion is a good idea.]

ANOTHER MEMBER [Seated]: Second!

CHAIR: It is moved and seconded that the Tennis League establish a division open to juniors and seniors enrolled in city high schools.

---

*The chair should *not* say, "You are out of order." In this case, it is the motion that is not in order, not the member. RONR (11th ed.), p. 39, ll. 24–28.

D. HOW THE GROUP CONSIDERS A MOTION

1. Debate on the Motion

When a main motion has been stated by the chair, it is said to be **pending**—or, commonly, "on the floor." It is then before the group for debate and action. **Debate** means discussion on the merits of the question—that is, whether the proposed action should or should not be taken.

Right after stating the question on a motion, the chair normally turns toward the maker of the motion to see if he or she wishes to be assigned the floor.

The next chapter tells more about debate, including how to limit it or end it altogether.

Debate

MEMBER A [Stands]: Madam President!

CHAIR: Mr. A.

MEMBER A: We need to bring young people into tennis to keep the sport alive. . . . [Sits when finished.]

MEMBER B [Stands *after* Member A sits]: Madam President!

CHAIR: Mrs. B.

MEMBER B: Most of our members are adults. High school students should establish their own league. . . . [Sits when finished.]

During debate, there are also certain other motions that you may make relating to the main motion's consideration, or, in some cases, interrupting its consideration. These are called **secondary motions**. For example, a motion to *Recess*, described in Chapter 2, is a secondary motion that *interrupts*. The most common secondary motion that *relates* to a pending motion is a motion to *Amend* it, which we will cover in Chapter 5. We will cover some other secondary motions later on; they are all treated in RONR. [RONR (11th ed.), pp. 42–44, 59–60.]

2. The Chair "Puts" the Question

When no one else seeks recognition to debate, the chair may ask, **"Are you ready for the question?"** (or **"Is there any further debate?"**) This means, "Is everyone in the group ready to vote on the proposal immediately, or does anyone first want to speak about it, or offer amendments or other motions related to it?" Then—if there is still no effort to get the floor for further debate—the chair stands and puts the question to a vote. [RONR (11th ed.), p. 37, l. 32 to p. 38, l. 1; p. 44, ll. 13–18.]

To do so, the chair begins by saying, **"The question is on the adoption of the motion that . . ."** and then repeats the exact wording of the motion to be voted on: for example, **"The question is on the adoption of the motion that** the Tennis League establish a division open to juniors and seniors enrolled in city high schools."

The chair then gives the necessary directions for the group to vote on the motion. Most motions require a majority of those present and voting to pass. Some require a two-thirds vote.* (**Abstentions**—instances in which members who are present do not vote—are not counted and have no effect on the result.)

The simplest and most common type of voting is the voice vote. The chair says, **"Those in favor of the motion, say *aye.*"** Those in support, remaining seated, then call out "aye." The chair then says, **"Those opposed, say *no.*"** The opponents, also seated, call out,

---

*Table D on pp. 194–95 lists the votes required for some common motions. A comprehensive list is found in RONR (11th ed.), tinted pages 6–29 (Table II).

"no." The chair judges whether more people called out "aye" or "no" and, based on this judgment, proceeds to announce the result of the vote. [RONR (11th ed.), pp. 44–47.]

Other methods of voting, including the procedure to be followed when the result of a voice vote is unclear, are covered in Chapter 8.

Putting the Question

CHAIR: The question is on the adoption of the motion that the Tennis League establish a division open to juniors and seniors enrolled in city high schools. Those in favor of the motion, say *aye*.

SOME MEMBERS [Seated]: Aye!

CHAIR: Those opposed, say *no*.

OTHER MEMBERS [Seated]: No!

---

3. The Chair Announces the Result of the Vote

When the voting is complete, the chair announces the result. Each announcement has three parts:

1) reporting which side "has it";
2) declaring that the motion is adopted or lost; and
3) indicating the effect of the vote, if needed or appropriate.

Immediately after announcing the result of the vote, the chair announces the next item of business, when applicable.

If there were more ayes than noes, the chair says, for example, "**The ayes have it, and the motion is adopted**. The Tennis League will establish a division open to juniors and seniors enrolled in city high schools. **The next item of business is . . ."** [*or*, if nothing is set automatically to come up next, **"Is there further new business?"**]

On the other hand, if the noes prevailed, the chair says, **"The noes have it and the motion is lost. The next item of business is . . ."** [*or*, if nothing is set automatically to come up next, **"Is there further new business?"**] [RONR (11th ed.), pp. 47–51.]

Announcement of Voting Result and the Business That Follows

CHAIR: The ayes have it, and the motion is adopted. The Tennis League will establish a division open to juniors and seniors enrolled in city high schools. Is there further new business?

OR

The noes have it, and the motion is lost. Is there further new business?

Review: Example of Handling a Simple Motion

MEMBER A [Stands]: Madam President!

CHAIR: Mr. A.

MEMBER A: I move that the Tennis League establish a division open to juniors and seniors enrolled in city high schools. [Sits when finished.]

ANOTHER MEMBER [Seated]: Second!

CHAIR: It is moved and seconded that the Tennis League establish a division open to juniors and seniors enrolled in city high schools.

MEMBER A [Stands]: Madam President!

(*continued on next page*)

Review: Example of Handling a Simple Motion (*continued*)

CHAIR: Mr. A.

MEMBER A: We need to bring young people into tennis to keep the sport alive. . . . [Sits.]

MEMBER B [Stands]: Madam President!

CHAIR: Mrs. B.

MEMBER B: Most of our members are adults. High school students should establish their own league. . . . [Sits when finished.]

CHAIR: Is there any further debate? . . . The question is on the adoption of the motion that the Tennis League establish a division open to juniors and seniors enrolled in city high schools. Those in favor of the motion, say *aye*.

SOME MEMBERS [Seated]: Aye!

CHAIR: Those opposed, say *no*.

OTHER MEMBERS [Seated]: No!

CHAIR: The ayes have it, and the motion is carried. The Tennis League will establish a division open to juniors and seniors enrolled in city high schools. Is there further new business?

OR

The noes have it, and the motion is lost. Is there further new business?

DEBATE

CHAPTER CONTENTS

A. THE RULES FOR DEBATE

1. Speech Limits in Debate

You may speak in debate twice on any debatable motion on the same day. Each time, you may speak for up to ten minutes. These limits apply to any organization that has not adopted special rules setting other limits, as many do.

You cannot "save" time or transfer it to someone else. So you cannot, for example, speak for five minutes your first time up and fifteen minutes the second time. Unlike the practice in Congress, you cannot "yield the floor" to let someone else speak on your time (except that you can choose to let people ask you questions on your time). [RONR (11th ed.), pp. 387–90.]

2. Who Gets Preference in Recognition to Debate?

As a general rule, the chair should designate to speak, or **recognize**, the person who rises first after the previous speaker has finished and sat down.

You *cannot*, while someone is still speaking, try to signal that you want to speak next. You must wait until the person who is speaking finishes and sits down before standing and seeking the chance to speak by calling out the chair's title.

There are three common exceptions to the rule that the person who rises first should be the one recognized to speak.

• First, if you are the maker of a motion, you have a one-time right to preference in speaking about it. Normally, the maker of the motion is the first to speak on it immediately after the chair has stated the motion.

- Second, although everyone may speak twice on the same motion on the same day, someone who has not yet spoken on it even once has preference over anyone who has already spoken on it.
- Third, when the chair knows that persons seeking the floor have opposite opinions on the motion, he or she should try to alternate between speakers who favor and those who oppose a proposal that is being debated. So if there has just been a speech in favor of the motion, someone who wants to speak against it then should, if possible, be given preference over another person wanting to support it.*

General Rule: A member can establish entitlement to the floor by rising first *after* it has been yielded.

(A member *cannot* establish entitlement to the floor by rising *before* it has been yielded.)

Common Exceptions

Maker of motion has one-time preference
One who has not yet spoken has preference
Alternate between supporters and opponents

---

3. Stick to the Subject

In debate, your speech must relate to the motion under discussion. The rule is that your remarks must be **germane**, that is, that they must have bearing on whether the pending motion should be adopted. Going off on irrelevant topics is not in order. [RONR (11th ed.), p. 392, ll. 5–10.]

---

*While these are the most common exceptions, there are a number of others. For the complete rules, see RONR (11th ed.), pages 378–83.

4. Debate Issues, Not Personalities

One of the most important rules of debate is that the proposal, not the member, is the subject of debate. Vigorous debate about the merits of a motion is central to the very idea of a deliberative assembly. When the arguments on all sides are fully aired, the group is most likely to come to a wise decision. Criticizing an opponent's reasoning, however, is different from criticizing the opponent personally.

If debate were allowed to include personal attacks, it might intimidate many from taking part in the debate who might otherwise make important points. It would certainly leave hard feelings and foster personal antipathy in the group long after the debate had ended and the group's decision had been made.

When a motion is pending, you may attack the idea or likely results of the proposal in strong terms, but *you must avoid personalities*! Under no circumstances can you attack or question the motives of another member. If you disagree with someone else's statement, you cannot say in debate that the statement "is false." You might instead say, "I believe there is strong evidence that the member is mistaken." Terms such as "fraud," "liar," or "lie" must never be used about a member in debate. [RONR (11th ed.), p. 392, ll. 12–25.]

5. Formalities That Avoid Personalities

To decrease the danger that debate will become personal, the rules of debate call for certain formalities of speech that may seem unusual to many people today.

The most important of these is that in debate you speak as though you are talking to the chair, not directly to other members. You don't say, "Jim, that argument you just made is ridiculous." Instead, you might say, "Mr. President, the last speaker's final point doesn't really make sense."

Even if you are asking a question of another person, do this through the chair. Instead of saying, "Juanita, how much money do we have left in the treasury?" you say, "Madam President, would the Treasurer please tell us how much money the Society has left in the treasury?"

Also, as much as possible avoid using the *names* of other members in debate. You should normally refer to the officers by their titles (for example, "in the Secretary's report"). Strictly speaking, the same is true of ordinary members: It is preferable to say "the previous speaker" instead of "Arthur Rothstein."

In practice, the degree of formality actually used often varies with the circumstances of the meeting and the nature of the group. [RONR (11th ed.), p. 392, l. 27 to p. 393, l. 10.]

B. MOTIONS THAT ARE AND ARE NOT DEBATABLE

Every main motion and some secondary motions may be debated. But there are other secondary motions which are not debatable. [RONR (11th ed.), pp. 396–99.]

For motions discussed in some detail in this book, whether or not they are debatable can be learned from the Table of Rules Relating to Motions in Table D on pages 194–95. For other motions, see Table II in RONR (11th ed.), tinted pages 6–29.

Example of Debate

CHAIR: It is moved and seconded that the Tennis League establish a division open to juniors and seniors enrolled in city high schools.

MEMBER B [Stands]: Madam President!

MEMBER A (maker of the motion) [Stands]: Madam President!

(continued on next page)

Example of Debate *(continued)*

CHAIR: Mr. A. [Member B sits.]

MEMBER A: We need to bring young people into tennis to keep the sport alive . . . . Please vote for this motion. [Sits when finished.]

MEMBER C [Stands]: Madam President!

MEMBER B [Stands]: Madam President!

MEMBER D [Stands]: Madam President!

CHAIR: Since the last speaker spoke in favor of the motion, who wishes to speak in opposition to the motion?

[MEMBER D sits.]

MEMBER C [Remaining standing]: Madam President!

MEMBER B [Remaining standing]: Madam President!

CHAIR: Mrs. C. [Member B sits.]

MEMBER C: Most of our members are adults. High school students should establish their own league . . . .

[Sits when finished.]

MEMBER A [Stands]: Madam President!

MEMBER D [Stands]: Madam President!

MEMBER E [Stands]: Madam President!

MEMBER B [Stands]: Madam President!

CHAIR: Mr. A. has already spoken once, and others who have not spoken wish to speak. [Member A sits.] Since the last speaker opposed the motion, who else wishes to speak in its favor? [Member B sits.]

MEMBER D [Remaining standing]: Madam President!

MEMBER E [Remaining standing]: Madam President!

(continued on next page)

Example of Debate (*continued*)

CHAIR: Mr. D. [Member E sits.]

MEMBER D: Madam President, we need young people to rejuvenate this sport . . . . [Sits when finished.]

MEMBER A [Stands]: Madam President!

CHAIR: Mr. A.

MEMBER A: Without outside help, it is unlikely high school students can afford to create a tennis league. In my opinion,

MEMBER B [Stands and interrupts]: Madam President, will the speaker yield for a question?

MEMBER A: I will be happy to yield for a question.

MEMBER B: How does the gentleman say we should pay for the student division he proposes? [Sits.]

MEMBER A: Madam President, the dues the high school students would pay should cover the costs of the division. To continue my argument . . . . [Sits when finished.]

C. LIMIT OR EXTEND LIMITS OF DEBATE

As we have seen, the general rule governing debate is that any member may speak up to twice a day on any debatable motion, and for up to ten minutes at a time. There is no other limit on the time taken for debate. If many members use their full right to speak under this rule, consideration of any motion can take a very long time.

It is possible to change these debate limits, but only by a two-thirds vote. A two-thirds vote is required as a compromise between the right of the individual to be heard and the right of the group not to be unduly delayed in conducting its business.

A motion to *Limit or Extend the Limits of Debate* might limit debate on the pending motion to one hour, or set a time when all debate will end and the question will be voted on. It might limit speeches to two minutes instead of ten. On the other hand, you could also use this motion to *increase* the number of times a member can speak from two to four, or the time allowed for each speech to 15 minutes.

Any combination of limits and extensions is also possible. For example, there might be a motion to allow members to speak up to three times for no more than two minutes each time.

A motion to *Limit or Extend the Limits of Debate* is itself undebatable.* The purpose of a motion that can limit debate would be defeated if opponents could endlessly debate the limitation itself. However, the motion can be amended (see Chapter 5) so as to change the specifics of the debate limits it proposes.

Some examples of such motions are:

"I move that in debate on the pending amendment, each member be limited to one speech of three minutes."

"I move that debate on the pending motion be limited to twenty minutes."

"I move that at 9 P.M. debate be closed and the question on the motion be put to a vote." [RONR (11th ed.), pp. 191–97, 390–91.]

D. CLOSE DEBATE IMMEDIATELY: THE MOTION FOR THE PREVIOUS QUESTION

Often you will want not just to limit debate, but to end it altogether. There is a specialized motion for this purpose. The adoption of this motion immediately closes debate and also prevents the making

---

*This is true unless the motion to limit debate is made while no other motion is pending. RONR (11th ed.), p. 192, ll. 1–7; tinted pp. 14–15, #31.

of a number of secondary motions, including those to *Amend*,* *Commit*, and *Postpone to a Certain Time*.** (Its adoption prevents the making of *further* motions of these types, but if any of them had already been stated, but not voted on, before adoption of the *Previous Question*, they must still be voted on by the group.) It may be moved at any time while a debatable motion is pending, whether or not some debate on it has already taken place.

The motion to close debate immediately is called the motion for the *Previous Question*.† Like the motion to *Limit or Extend the Limits of Debate*, the motion for the *Previous Question* requires a two-thirds vote, and is undebatable.

The proper wording to close debate on the immediately pending motion is to say, **"I move the previous question."**

Because it closes debate and brings the assembly to an immediate vote, something that is frequently desired or necessary, the motion for the *Previous Question* is quite commonly used in meetings. Frequently, however, the motion is made in a nonstandard form, by a member saying, "I call the question," or "I move we vote now." If otherwise properly moved, the chair should treat these as motions for the *Previous Question*. [RONR (11th ed.), p. 202, ll. 3–10.]

Sometimes a member will call out, "Question!" or "Vote!" without first seeking recognition and obtaining the floor. This does *not* qualify as the making of the motion, and is out of order if another member is speaking or seeking recognition. [RONR (11th ed.), p. 207, ll. 18–20.]

Cutting off debate infringes on the right of members to speak. Therefore, no one member or group of members can force an immediate end to debate if even one member with the right to do so

---

*Amendments are explained in Chapter 5.

**Commit* and *Postpone to a Certain Time* are covered in Chapter 6.

†The name of this specialized motion, the *Previous Question*, comes from its usage in the British Parliament. The meaning of the motion here has nothing to do with any question previously considered by the assembly.

wants to speak, except through the proper adoption of the *Previous Question*. This requires seeking and getting recognition and then moving the *Previous Question*, after which it must be seconded and adopted by a two-thirds vote. [RONR (11th ed.), pp. 197–209.]

Example of the Previous Question

MEMBER A [standing]: Mr. President!

CHAIR: Member A.

MEMBER A: I move the previous question. [Sits.]

ANOTHER MEMBER [Seated]: Second!

CHAIR: It is moved and seconded to order the previous question. [The chair may explain that ordering the previous question will cut off any further debate.] Those in favor of ordering the previous question will rise.

SOME STAND

Be seated. Those opposed will rise.

OTHERS STAND

Be seated. There are two thirds in the affirmative and the previous question is ordered. The question is now on the adoption of the motion to [stating in full the immediately pending question]. Those in favor, say *aye*. [The chair proceeds to complete the vote on the underlying motion.]

AMENDMENTS

CHAPTER CONTENTS

A. THE PURPOSE AND CONSTRUCTION OF AMENDMENTS

When a group is debating a main motion, such as "That the Tennis League establish a division open to juniors and seniors enrolled in city high schools," you may think the proposal can be improved if it is changed in some way.

You may like the idea of a student division, but think it should be limited to seniors. You may believe that not only city high school students, but also those from adjoining counties, should be eligible. You may think that the students should be part of the regular league rather than members of a separate division.

To try to get the group to agree with these ideas, you can propose **amendments**—which, if adopted, modify the wording and, within limits, often the meaning of the main motion.

Amendments should say *exactly* where in the main motion the change is to be made, and *precisely* what words to use. Put an amendment together just as if you were giving detailed, word-by-word directions to the secretary how to change the main motion. So *don't* say something like, "I move to amend so that students from suburban counties can also join." Instead, say, "I move to amend by inserting 'and suburban county' before 'high schools.'"

The chair can, and often should, require that amendments, like main motions, be submitted by the mover in writing. [RONR (11th ed.), p. 40, ll. 4–7.]

The vote on your amendment does *not* decide whether the main motion will be adopted, only whether the wording in the main motion will be changed. After an amendment is adopted, the main motion as amended may be further debated and further amended. In the end, a vote is taken on the main motion *as amended*. Only if the motion passes on that vote will the group finally decide to do what your amendment—together with the rest of the main motion—proposes to do. [RONR (11th ed.), p. 131, ll. 3–5.]

B. SIMPLE WORD CHANGES

The basic rules for amendments that make simple word changes are not very difficult to understand. There are three types of these amendments.

1. Insert or Add Words

Suppose that you want to allow suburban county high school students to join, as well as city high school students.

The main motion is:
"That the Tennis League establish a division open to juniors and seniors enrolled in city high schools."
You want the motion to read:
"That the Tennis League establish a division open to juniors and seniors enrolled in city *and suburban county* high schools."

This requires inserting the words "and suburban county" *before the words* "high schools."

You may do this with an amendment *to insert words*. After being recognized by the chair when no one else is speaking, you say, "**I move to insert the words** 'and suburban county' **before the words** 'high schools.'" (If you wanted words to be put at the end of the motion, that would call for an amendment *to add words* and you would say, for example, "**I move to add the words** 'and those in suburban county high schools.'") [RONR (11th ed.), p. 139, l. 34 to p. 141, l. 9; p. 141, ll. 26–36.]

If some other member seconds your amendment, the chair states it, and then you can seek recognition again to speak for the amendment. After any further debate, the chair puts the question on your amendment, and the group votes.

In the following example, note how the chair, in stating and then putting the question, ensures that the members know exactly what is under consideration. The chair:

1) states the amendment;
2) gives the main motion as it would read if the amendment were to be adopted; and
3) makes clear once more what is the *amendment* that is to be debated or voted on.

In announcing the result of the vote on the amendment, the chair finishes by restating the wording of the main motion as it then stands. [RONR (11th ed.), p. 142, l. 1 to p. 144, l. 14.]

Handling an Amendment to Insert Words

CHAIR: The question is on the adoption of the motion: "That the Tennis League establish a division open to juniors and seniors enrolled in city high schools."

MEMBER A [Stands]: Madam President!

CHAIR: Mrs. A.

MEMBER A: I move to insert the words "and suburban county" before the words "high schools." [Sits when finished.]

ANOTHER MEMBER [Seated]: Second!

CHAIR: It is moved and seconded to insert the words "and suburban county" before the words "high schools." If the

---

(continued on next page)

Handling an Amendment to Insert Words *(continued)*

> amendment is adopted, the main motion will read, "That the Tennis League establish a division open to juniors and seniors enrolled in city and suburban county high schools." The question is on inserting the words "and suburban county."
>
> [Debate.]
>
> CHAIR: Are you ready for the question? . . . The question is on inserting the words "and suburban county" before the words "high schools." If the amendment is adopted, the main motion will read, "That the Tennis League establish a division open to juniors and seniors enrolled in city and suburban county high schools." Those in favor of inserting the words "and suburban county," say *aye*.
>
> SOME MEMBERS [Seated]: Aye!
>
> CHAIR: Those opposed, say *no*.
>
> OTHER MEMBERS [Seated]: No!
>
> CHAIR: The ayes have it, and the amendment is adopted. The question is now on the main motion as amended, "That the Tennis League establish a division open to juniors and seniors enrolled in city and suburban county high schools." Is there any further debate?

2. Strike Out Words

Suppose you believe the new student division should be open to high school seniors, but not juniors.

The main motion is:

"That the Tennis League establish a division open to juniors and seniors enrolled in city and suburban county high schools."

You want the motion to read:

"That the Tennis League establish a division open to ~~juniors and~~ seniors enrolled in city and suburban county high schools."

This requires getting rid of the two words "juniors and."

You can do this by an *amendment to strike out words*. During the debate on the main motion, when no one is speaking, you seek recognition, and if the chair gives you the floor, you say, "**I move to strike out the words** 'juniors and.'" [RONR (11th ed.), pp. 146–47, 148–49.]

Handling an Amendment to Strike Out Words

CHAIR: The question is on the adoption of the motion, "That the Tennis League establish a division open to juniors and seniors enrolled in city and suburban county high schools."

MEMBER A [Stands]: Madam President!

CHAIR: Mr. A.

MEMBER A: I move to strike out the words "juniors and." [Sits when finished.]

ANOTHER MEMBER [Seated]: Second!

CHAIR: It is moved and seconded to strike out the words "juniors and." If the amendment is adopted, the motion

---

(continued on next page)

Handling an Amendment to Strike Out Words *(continued)*

will read, "That the Tennis League establish a division open to seniors enrolled in city and suburban county high schools." The question is on striking the words "juniors and."

[Debate.]

CHAIR: Is there any further debate? . . . The question is on striking out the words "juniors and." If the amendment is adopted, the main motion will read, "That the Tennis League establish a division open to seniors enrolled in city and suburban county high schools." Those in favor of striking the words "juniors and," say *aye.*

SOME MEMBERS [Seated]: Aye!

CHAIR: Those opposed, say *no.*

OTHER MEMBERS [Seated]: No!

CHAIR: The ayes have it, and the amendment is adopted. The question is now on the main motion as amended, "That the Tennis League establish a division open to seniors enrolled in city and suburban county high schools." Is there any further debate?

3. Strike Out and Insert Words

The third type of motion to amend words combines the motion to strike out words and the motion to insert, or add, words. Suppose you think the high school students should be members of the regular Tennis League, not members of a separate division.

The main motion is:
"That the Tennis League establish a division open to seniors enrolled in city and suburban county high schools."

You want the motion to read:
"That the Tennis League ~~establish a division open to~~ *accept as members* seniors enrolled in city and suburban county high schools."

This requires striking out the words "establish a division open to" *and inserting the words* "accept as members."

You obtain recognition and say, "**I move to strike out the words** 'establish a division open to' **and insert the words** 'accept as members.'" [RONR (11th ed.), pp. 149–53.]

Handling an Amendment to Strike Out and Insert Words

CHAIR: The question is on the adoption of the motion, "That the Tennis League establish a division open to seniors enrolled in city and suburban county high schools."

MEMBER A [Stands]: Madam President!

CHAIR: Mrs. A.

MEMBER A: I move to strike out the words "establish a division open to" and insert the words "accept as members." [Sits when finished.]

ANOTHER MEMBER [Seated]: Second!

(continued on next page)

Handling an Amendment to Strike Out and Insert Words *(continued)*

CHAIR: It is moved and seconded to strike out the words "establish a division open to" and insert the words "accept as members." If the amendment is adopted, the main motion will read, "That the Tennis League accept as members seniors enrolled in city and suburban county high schools." The question is on striking out the words "establish a division open to" and inserting the words "accept as members."

[Debate.]

CHAIR: Is there any further debate? . . . The question is on striking out the words "establish a division open to" and inserting the words "accept as members." If the amendment is adopted, the main motion will read, "That the Tennis League accept as members seniors enrolled in city and suburban county high schools." Those in favor of striking out the words "establish a division open to" and inserting the words "accept as members," say *aye*.

SOME MEMBERS [Seated]: Aye!

CHAIR: Those opposed, say *no*.

OTHER MEMBERS [Seated]: No!

CHAIR: The noes have it, and the amendment is lost. The question is now on the main motion as previously amended, which is, "That the Tennis League establish a division open to seniors enrolled in city and suburban county high schools." Is there any further debate?

C. AMENDING PARAGRAPHS

We have seen that there are three forms of amendment that apply to words: insert, or add, words; strike out words; and strike out and insert words. There are also three forms of amendment that apply to whole paragraphs (or larger units) that roughly parallel the three forms of amendment that apply to words.

1. Insert or Add a Paragraph

The rules that apply to inserting or adding a paragraph or paragraphs are largely identical to those that apply to inserting or adding words. A motion to insert or add paragraphs may also insert or add larger units that may consist of many paragraphs, such as an article or a section. [RONR (11th ed.), p. 141.]

2. Strike Out a Paragraph

It is possible to offer a motion to strike out an entire paragraph, or paragraphs. An amendment to strike out paragraphs may cover larger units, such as sections or articles. [RONR (11th ed.), pp. 147–49.]

3. Substitute

The form for amending paragraphs that parallels striking out and inserting words has its own name: *to substitute*. A **substitute** replaces a paragraph or paragraphs in the immediately pending motion with one or more paragraphs given in the amendment. A substitute may be offered for a paragraph or paragraphs, or any larger units: sections, articles, or even an entire main motion. [RONR (11th ed.), pp. 153–62.]

To illustrate, take the example of the main motion we have been using.

The main motion is:

"That the Tennis League establish a division open to seniors enrolled in city and suburban county high schools."

You want the motion to read:

"That high school students be encouraged to take up the sport of tennis, and to form their own league for practice and competitive play."

This involves offering a different paragraph as a substitute for the pending motion.

Handling a Substitute

MEMBER F [Stands]: Mr. President!

CHAIR: Mrs. F.

MEMBER F: I move to substitute for the pending motion the following: "That high school students be encouraged to take up the sport of tennis, and to form their own league for practice and competitive play." [Sits.]

MEMBER G [remaining seated]: Second!

CHAIR: It is moved and seconded to amend by substituting for the pending motion the following: "That high school students be encouraged to take up the sport of tennis, and to form their own league for practice and competitive play." The motion to substitute proposes that the paragraph just read shall come before the assembly in place of the pending motion.

(continued on next page)

Handling a Substitute (*continued*)

[Debate.]

CHAIR: Are you ready for the question on the motion to substitute? . . . The question is on the motion to substitute. The chair will read the pending motion first, then the motion proposed as a substitute. The pending motion is: "That the Tennis League establish a division open to seniors enrolled in city and suburban county high schools." The motion proposed as a substitute is: "That high school students be encouraged to take up the sport of tennis, and to form their own league for practice and competitive play." The question is: Shall the motion last read be substituted for the pending motion? Those in favor of the motion to substitute, say *aye*.

SOME MEMBERS [remaining seated]: Aye!

CHAIR: Those opposed, say *no*.

OTHER MEMBERS [remaining seated]: No!

CHAIR: The ayes have it and the motion to substitute is adopted. The question is now on the main motion as amended: "That high school students be encouraged to take up the sport of tennis, and to form their own league for practice and competitive play." Are you ready for the question?

D. AMENDING AMENDMENTS

An amendment to a main motion may itself be amended by a "secondary amendment," sometimes called an "amendment of the second degree" or an "amendment to the amendment." The rules for secondary amendments, which can get complex, are covered in

RONR (11th ed.), pages 130–62. Secondary amendments may not themselves be amended—there can be no "third degree" or "tertiary" amendments, because they would be too confusing.

Instead of proposing a secondary amendment, one simple approach is to tell the group that if it will vote down the pending amendment, you will then offer a different version, which you may then describe. [RONR (11th ed.), p. 135, ll. 22–26; p. 152, ll. 13–27.]

E. STICKING TO THE SUBJECT: THE GERMANENESS RULE

Any amendment proposed must *in some way involve* the same question raised by the motion it amends. This is known as the requirement that an amendment must be **germane**. (We have already covered the similar rule that debate must be germane to the pending motion, on page 30.)

If the main motion is, "That the Tennis League establish a division open to seniors enrolled in city and suburban county high schools," an amendment to add "and oppose any city tax increase" would not be germane. It would not be in order because opposition to a tax increase does not relate to or involve the motion establishing a division for students. [RONR (11th ed.), pp. 136–38.]

F. THE "SETTLED" RULE

The time of the group should not be wasted by making it vote over and over again on the same thing. So once the group has voted on an amendment, that specific matter is considered settled.* If the

---

*There are ways a group can go back and change something it has already decided, but often only through special motions with their own rules. See Chapter 7.

group has voted down an amendment to add certain words, you cannot propose another amendment to add substantially the same words in the same place.

For the same reason, if the group has adopted an amendment to insert certain words, a later amendment that would change just those words is not in order. However, it is sometimes possible to propose an amendment that takes "a bigger bite"—one that amends the main motion in a way that changes parts of the motion that have not previously been amended *together with* the words that were earlier inserted.

The basic rule is that after the group has voted that certain words shall, or shall not, be part of a motion, you cannot offer another amendment that raises the same question of content and effect. Common sense is necessary to apply this principle from case to case. [RONR (11th ed.), p. 139, ll. 23–33.]

POSTPONING
AND REFERRING
TO A COMMITTEE

CHAPTER CONTENTS

A. POSTPONE TO A
CERTAIN TIME

Suppose that you are in the middle of debate on a main motion, and you want to put off taking a vote on it. Perhaps it is a matter that is not urgent, and you want to take up something which is. Perhaps you feel more information is needed, and want time to gather it, before making a decision. There could be a hundred reasons why you might want to stop dealing with a proposal for the time being and put it off until another occasion.

The motion to *Postpone to a Certain Time* meets this need. If adopted by a majority vote, it puts off further consideration of the main motion to a later time or meeting named in the motion. For example:

I move to postpone the motion until 3 P.M.
OR
I move to postpone the motion to the next meeting. (In this case it will come up right after unfinished business at the next meeting.*)

After a motion to *Postpone to a Certain Time* has been stated, it may itself be amended, for example to change the time to which the main motion is to be postponed. It is also debatable, but the debate must be limited to the *motion* to *Postpone*. This means you may talk about whether it is or is not a good idea to postpone the main motion, or about the details of the postponement, such as for how long

---

*The full name of the class of business described in this book as "Unfinished Business" is actually "Unfinished Business and General Orders," and an item postponed to the next meeting in this manner is an example of a "general order." The topic of general orders is somewhat complicated, and is covered in RONR (11th ed.); see p. 358, l. 1 to p. 360, l. 12 and p. 364, l. 17 to p. 369, l. 10. See also p. 185, l. 29 to p. 187, l. 15.

it should be. However, you may *not* debate whether the main motion itself is good or bad.

In the ordinary circumstance, you cannot postpone a motion beyond the next regular meeting, and not beyond the third month after the present month. For example, at a meeting in February, a motion can't be postponed to a meeting later than in May, even if that is the next regular meeting. [RONR (11th ed.), pp. 179–91.]

B. COMMIT OR REFER

Before voting on a main motion, you may feel that it would profit from redrafting or further study by a small group of people. It may be that much time would be required to amend the main motion properly, or that additional information is needed, so that it would be best to turn the motion over to a committee for study or redrafting before the full group considers it further.

The motion to *Commit* (*Refer* to a committee) allows this. It requires a majority vote, and should identify the committee to which the motion is to be referred. It may include instructions to the committee; for example, it may specify when the committee is to report, or that the committee shall propose an amendment written to accomplish a particular purpose.

Committees are of two basic types. **Standing committees** have a continuing existence and function, normally responsibility over a particular subject matter: for example, the Education Committee, or the Membership Committee. If a motion's content falls within the subject matter of a standing committee, it must be referred—if it is to be sent to a committee at all—to that committee.

A motion to refer to a standing committee might be:

> **"I move that the motion be referred to** the Fundraising Committee, and that the committee be instructed to report at the August meeting."

Special committees are created for a particular task, and go out of existence when that task is completed. For example, if a main motion to purchase a new headquarters is pending, you may want to refer it to a specially created committee with instructions to study the proposal and report the committee's recommendations at the next meeting.

A motion to refer to a special committee might be:

> **"I move to refer the motion to a committee** of seven, the chairman to be Mr. Adams, with six additional members to be appointed by the president, and to instruct the committee to report at the August meeting."

The motion to *Commit* is amendable: for example, to change any proposed instructions to the committee, or to change the makeup of a special committee. It is also debatable. Debate must be about the desirability of referring the matter to the committee, or about the details of the referral (which committee, when to report, and so forth). While the motion to commit is pending, you may *not* debate whether the main motion itself is good or bad. [RONR (11th ed.), pp. 168–79.]

C. HOW COMMITTEE MEMBERS ARE CHOSEN

1. Standing Committees

The method of selection of the chairmen and members of standing committees is usually established in the organization's bylaws.* Normally, bylaws provide either that the members of standing committees are appointed by the president at the beginning of his or her term of office or that they are elected by the group at the same meeting at which the group's officers are elected. Members of standing committees generally serve for the same period as the officers of the organization.

2. Special Committees

As we have seen, special committees are created for a particular purpose. A motion to refer a pending motion to a special committee itself creates the special committee. If no motion is pending, a special committee may also be created by a main motion that assigns a particular subject or matter to the committee. If the bylaws are silent on the method of appointing members of special committees, the method is typically set for that committee in the motion creating the committee.** One common method is to provide that the members of the special committee be appointed by the presiding officer. Another is for the motion itself to name the members. The sample motion in the second box on page 55 illustrates a combination of these methods.[†]

---

*Bylaws are explained in Chapter 10.

**If the motion to commit does not establish how the committee is to be appointed, then after its adoption the assembly, guided by the presiding officer, must vote on how this is to be done. RONR (11th ed.), p. 173, l. 24 to p. 174, l. 29.

[†]RONR (11th ed.), pp. 492–96. For procedure in committees and committee reports, see Chapter 19.

CHAPTER 7

HOW CAN A GROUP CHANGE ITS MIND?

CHAPTER CONTENTS

A. CORRECTING MISTAKES

A meeting might never end if those who were defeated in one vote could repeatedly try to overturn the decision by making the group vote on the same matter over and over. For this reason, it's a rule of parliamentary procedure that once a motion has come up and been disposed of at a meeting, another motion that raises the same question can't be brought up at the same meeting in the normal way.* Another important principle is that, as a protection against instability—arising, for example, from such factors as slight variations in attendance—the requirements for changing a previous action are generally greater than those for taking the action in the first place.

But every once in a while—either after reflection or because you learn of new facts—you may come to the conclusion that maybe the group did something it should not have done or should have done differently, or that it made a mistake in choosing not to do something it should have done. There are special procedures for dealing with such cases in meetings.

B. THE MOTION TO RECONSIDER

If a motion has been either adopted or defeated during a meeting, and at least one member who voted on the winning side wants to have the vote reconsidered, such a member may make the motion to *Reconsider*.

This motion can *only* be made by a member who voted on the winning side. That is to say, if the motion was adopted, the motion to *Reconsider* can be made only by a member who voted in favor of

---

*The same is true during a series of connected meetings called a **session**—for example, a convention lasting several days. In an ordinary club each meeting is usually a separate session. RONR (11th ed.), pp. 81–88.

the motion, or if the motion was defeated, then only by a member who voted against it. This makes sense because, if there is no such person, there is virtually no chance that the result of the vote will be any different on the second go-round. This motion can, however, be seconded by any member, no matter how he or she voted.

Another important thing that you must know about *Reconsider* is that there is only a limited period of time within which it can be made. In the usual case, this motion can be made only on the same day on which the vote sought to be reconsidered was taken. The only exception to this rule is in the case of a session (such as a lengthy convention) in which meetings take place over a period of more than one day. In that event, the motion to *Reconsider* can be made on the same day the original vote was taken or on the next succeeding day within the session on which a business meeting is held. By and large, however, the thing for you to keep in mind is that if you change your mind after the meeting is over, in the usual situation you can forget about the motion to *Reconsider*. It will be too late to make such a motion.

Let's assume that, at a meeting, a motion is made to make a contribution of $500 to some worthy charity. You are concerned that there is not enough money for this purpose, and for that reason you vote against the motion. Other members apparently have similar concerns, because the motion is defeated. Later during the meeting, maybe because of additional information you have received, you change your mind and decide that the contribution really ought to be made, and you think that perhaps other members may have changed their minds as well.

If so, you may then make a motion to *Reconsider* the vote that defeated the motion to make the contribution. When you make this motion to *Reconsider*, remember to tell the presiding officer that you voted against the adoption of the motion relating to the contribution, so that it will be clear that you are entitled to make a motion to reconsider. You might say something like:

> **"Madam President, I move to reconsider the vote on the motion relating to** the contribution to the XYZ Charity. **I voted against that motion."**

If your motion to *Reconsider* is seconded, the chair will then state the question on your motion,* and the assembly will then proceed to consider the question of whether or not the motion concerning the contribution should be reconsidered. After any debate, a vote will be taken on the motion to *Reconsider*. If it is adopted by a majority vote, the motion to make the contribution will be back again before the assembly, just as it was before the original vote on it was taken. If a sufficient number of members have changed their minds after whatever further debate may take place, the motion to make the contribution may well be adopted this time. [RONR (11th ed.), pp. 315–32.]

C. THE MOTIONS TO RESCIND OR AMEND SOMETHING PREVIOUSLY ADOPTED

Suppose, however, that after a meeting is over (so that it is too late to move to reconsider) you feel that the assembly made the wrong decision when it adopted some motion.

For example, assume the assembly has adopted a resolution authorizing the purchase of certain property, which you now think was a mistake. At the next meeting (assuming, of course, that the property has not already been purchased), you may make a motion to *Rescind* the approval of the purchase. You might say something like:

---

*Unless another motion is pending at the time. See RONR (11th ed.), p. 316, l. 32 to p. 317, l. 15; pp. 323–24.

> **"I move to rescind the motion relating to** the purchase of the Smith farm property which was adopted at our June meeting."

Alternatively, if you are concerned only that too much money may be spent for this purchase, you may make a motion to *Amend Something Previously Adopted.* You might say:

> **"I move to amend** the authorization previously adopted to purchase the Smith farm property by adding 'provided, however, that the cost shall not exceed $200,000.00.'"

You may make either of these motions regardless of how you voted on the original motion, and there is no time limit on making either of them.

Both of these motions are main motions, and in most respects are treated like any other main motion. However, there is an important difference between them and other main motions in the vote needed to adopt them.

If *previous notice is not given* of an intent to make one of these motions, so that members are not alerted ahead of time to the fact that the motion will be made, adoption of the motion requires either

a) a two-thirds vote, or
b) the vote of a majority of the entire membership of the voting body,

whichever of these is the smaller number at the time.

If *previous notice is given,* however, a majority vote is all that is required for adoption. **Previous notice** of a motion is given either:

a) by announcing an intent to make such a motion at the meeting immediately preceding the meeting at which the motion is to be made; or

b) by having the secretary include notice of that intent in the **call** of the meeting at which the motion is to be made. This is the written notice of the time and place of the meeting, which is sent to members in advance of the meeting. [See p. 143 in this book.]

Therefore, if you know that you are going to want to make either of these motions, make every effort to give previous notice of your intent to do so. You will then need only a majority vote in order to succeed. [RONR (11th ed.), pp. 305–10.]

D. RENEWAL OF MOTIONS

Making a motion again after it has been defeated is called **renewal** of the motion.

As is obvious from the names of the motions to *Rescind* or *Amend Something Previously Adopted*, these motions only relate to things that have been *adopted*. What, however, if the matter concerns a motion that was defeated?

Suppose, for example, a motion to make a contribution of $500 to a worthy charity is defeated at one of your monthly meetings. You cannot simply make the same motion again at the same meeting. But after the meeting is over (so that it is too late to move to *Reconsider*), if you feel that the assembly has made the wrong decision and the motion to make the contribution should have been adopted, the solution is very simple. All you need to do is make the same motion again at your next monthly meeting. You can do this regardless of how you voted on the original motion. [RONR (11th ed.), pp. 336–37.]

Part III

VOTING AND ELECTIONS

CHAPTER

8

VOTING

CHAPTER CONTENTS

A. WHAT VOTE IS REQUIRED

1. Majority Vote

A **majority vote** is normally required to adopt a motion or to elect to office.* It is defined as "*more than half* of the votes cast by persons entitled to vote, excluding blanks or abstentions, at a regular or properly called meeting." [RONR (11th ed.), p. 400, ll. 7–12; see also q. 4 on pp. 114–15 and q. 6 on pp. 115–16 of this book.]

There may be fewer votes cast than the number of members present, since some may choose *not* to vote—resulting in "abstentions." Only a majority of those *actually voting* is required. If, for example, there are 10 members present at a meeting, and 4 vote in favor of a motion, while 3 vote against it, the 4 votes in favor are a majority of the 7 votes cast, and the motion is therefore adopted.

A majority vote is different from a **plurality vote**, which is the largest number of votes (which may be less than a majority) when there are three or more alternatives. If Fernandez gets 45 votes, Brubeck gets 40 votes, and Roscoe gets 15 votes, Fernandez has a plurality (more votes than anyone else), but has fallen short of a majority of the 100 votes cast, which would require more than 50 votes.

You are probably familiar with plurality votes (even if not by that name), since in the United States they are used for elections to Congress and usually for other legislative and executive offices. This means that when there are more than two candidates, it is possible for someone to be elected although getting less than a majority of the votes.

Under RONR, however, plurality votes are *not* sufficient; decisions require a majority vote. Therefore, in an election in which no candidate gets a majority, the vote must be repeated until one does

---

*Table D on pages 194–95 lists the vote required for common motions. A more comprehensive list is found in Table II of RONR (11th ed.), tinted pages 6–29.

get a majority. No candidate is dropped in the re-votes (unless he or she chooses to withdraw). The candidate with the lowest number in the first vote may turn out to be a "dark horse" on whom all factions may ultimately prefer to agree. [RONR (11th ed.), p. 404, l. 35 to p. 405, l. 14; p. 441, ll. 5–10.]

Regardless of whether the vote required is a majority vote or something else (such as a two-thirds vote as defined in the next paragraph), substantive actions can be validly taken only when a quorum is present, as previously stated on pages 12–13.

2. Two-Thirds Vote

A **two-thirds vote** is required in particular circumstances, most notably to suspend the rules (see Chapter 11) or to close, limit, or extend the limits of debate (see Chapter 4). It is defined as "*at least two thirds* of the votes cast by persons entitled to vote, excluding blanks or abstentions, at a regular or properly called meeting." [RONR (11th ed.), p. 401, ll. 8–17; see also q. 5 on p. 115 of this book.]

3. Majority of the Entire Membership

In some cases—such as when adopting a motion to *Rescind* or one to *Amend Something Previously Adopted* (covered in the previous chapter)—a vote of a **majority of the entire membership** is an allowable alternative. It is defined as "a majority of the total number of those who are members of the voting body at the time of the vote." [RONR (11th ed.), p. 403, ll. 25–27.]

The phrase "entire membership" means *all* members of the voting body, whether they are present at the meeting or not. In an organization which has both a general membership and a board, at a board meeting this means a majority of the entire membership of the board, not of the whole organization.

B. "UNANIMOUS CONSENT" INSTEAD OF A VOTE

As you probably noticed when reading Chapter 3, the complete process involved in the handling of a motion, from making the motion through announcement of the voting result, can be time-consuming. It would quickly become a nuisance if it were always necessary to go through the entire process for routine matters, particularly in instances when there seems to be no opposition. In such cases, a procedure known as **unanimous consent** can be used.

Unanimous consent enables a motion to be adopted or some action to be taken without the necessity of having the chair state the question on a motion and put the motion to a vote. It even permits taking action without the formality of a motion being made at all. The chair simply asks the assembly if there is any objection to taking the desired action, and if no member then objects, the chair declares that the action has been agreed to.

For example, suppose that a speaker whose time has expired in debate on a motion asks for two additional minutes. Instead of treating this as a formal motion for an extension of time (as discussed on pages 93–94), the chair may simply ask, **"Is there any objection to** the member's time being extended two minutes?" The chair then pauses, and if no member calls out **"I object,"** says something like, **"The chair hears no objection, and** the member's time is extended two minutes." It's as simple as that. However, if any member does call out an objection in response to the chair's question, the chair must then state the question on the motion and follow the rest of the complete, formal process for the handling of a motion.

A still more streamlined procedure, if the chair feels there is little chance of objection, is for him or her merely to say, **"Without objection,** the member's time is extended two minutes," and then proceed unless a member interrupts with an objection, which any member has the right to do. [RONR (11th ed.), pp. 54–56.]

C. MEMBERS' RIGHT TO VOTE

Any member whose right to vote has not been suspended as the result of a formal disciplinary process has the right to vote, even if his or her dues have not been paid. You *should not* vote on a question in which you have a direct personal or pecuniary (monetary) interest not common to other members. However, you *cannot be compelled* to abstain because of such a conflict of interest. [RONR (11th ed.), pp. 406–7.]

D. CHAIR'S PARTICIPATION IN VOTING

The presiding officer should make every effort to maintain an appearance of impartiality so that members on both sides of any issue can feel confident that they will receive fair treatment.*

To this end, the chair does not participate in debate on any issue unless he or she gives up the chair until the issue is disposed of (which should seldom be done). In addition, the chair votes only when either:

a) the vote is by ballot, in which case the chair votes along with and at the same time as all other members, or
b) the chair's vote will change the result of the vote.

If a motion requires a majority vote, it fails when there is a tie vote. Therefore, if there is a tie before the chair votes, the chair may announce that he or she is voting in the affirmative, causing the motion to be adopted.

---

*The rules restricting the chair's participation in voting and debate do not apply in meetings of committees or small boards. See pp. 158, 162.

If, following a vote, *the affirmative exceeds the negative by only one vote*, the chair may announce that he or she is voting in the negative, causing the motion to fail by creating a tie.

If the vote is on a motion that requires a two-thirds vote, the same rule applies. The rule is that the chair may vote if, by doing so, the outcome of the vote will change, either from adoption to rejection or from rejection to adoption.* So, if there is one *less* than two thirds in the affirmative, the chair might vote in the affirmative, so that the motion passes. On the other hand, if there are *exactly* two thirds in the affirmative, the chair might vote in the negative, so that there are then less than two thirds in the affirmative, and the motion fails. [RONR (11th ed.), pp. 405–6.]

E. MORE METHODS OF VOTING

Voting by voice, the most common method of voting, was described in Chapter 3. In addition, there are a few other methods that are frequently used.

1. Standing Vote

An *uncounted* standing vote is used in three cases.

1) Whenever a two-thirds vote, instead of a majority vote, is required to pass a motion, the chair should take a standing vote—*never* a voice vote.
2) Whenever the chair is not sure of the result of a voice vote, he or she should order a standing vote.
3) When you, as a member, reasonably doubt the result of a vote by voice or by show of hands, you have the right to demand that

---

*The wording used by the chair in these cases is given in Table A, on page 190.

the vote be re-taken as a standing vote simply by calling out, **"Division!"** As with seconding a motion, this may be done from your seat, without first obtaining the floor. The chair then says, **"A division is called for"** and proceeds to give directions for a standing vote.

To direct a division or standing vote, the chair says, **"Those in favor of the motion will rise. [Pause.] Be seated. Those opposed will rise. [Pause.] Be seated."**
Without actually counting, the chair judges whether more stood in the affirmative or the negative, and announces the result of the vote: for example, **"The affirmative has it, and the motion is adopted."**
OR: **"The negative has it and the motion is lost."** [RONR (11th ed.), pp. 46–47; p. 50, ll. 7–9; pp. 280–82.]

2. Show of Hands

In a small group a show of hands may be used instead of a voice or standing vote. The chair says, **"The question is on the adoption of the motion to** [repeating the exact words of the motion]. **Those in favor of the motion will raise the right hand. [Pause.] Lower hands. Those opposed will raise the right hand. [Pause.] Lower hands."** *Without actually counting*, the chair judges whether more hands were raised in the affirmative or the negative. The chair then announces the result of the vote, in the same way as after a standing vote. [RONR (11th ed.), pp. 47, 50; p. 409, ll. 32–36.]

3. Counted Vote

The methods of voting described so far rely on the chair's judging, without actually counting, whether there are more in favor or opposed to a motion (or, in some cases, whether at least two thirds favor it). If the chair is unsure of the results, he or she may re-take the vote as a standing counted vote. (Sometimes, in a small group, there can be a counted show of hands instead.) If the chair expects a vote to be close or the result to be challenged, he or she may choose to take a counted vote to begin with.

The group as a whole may direct that a vote be counted. A motion for a counted rising vote may be made while the motion on which that vote is sought is before the group. It may even be made immediately after a voice or uncounted rising vote has been taken, before any debate or business has intervened. After obtaining recognition, you say, **"I move that the vote be counted."** [RONR (11th ed.), p. 410, ll. 13–35.]

When a vote is to be counted, the chair says, **"Those in favor of the motion will rise and remain standing until counted.** [Pause for count.] **Be seated. Those opposed will rise and remain standing until counted.** [Pause for count.] **Be seated."** Depending on the size of the group, the counting may be done by the chair, with or without the chair directing the secretary to take an independent count for verification, or by **tellers** appointed by the chair. [RONR (11th ed.), p. 47, ll. 4–10; p. 411, ll. 1–21.]

The chair then announces, for example, **"There are 32 in the affirmative and 30 in the negative. The affirmative has it and the motion is adopted."**

OR: **"There are 30 in the affirmative and 30 in the negative. The negative has it and the motion is lost."** [RONR (11th ed.), pp. 50–51.]

Illustration: Voice, Standing, and Counted Vote

CHAIR: Is there any further debate? . . . The question is on the adoption of the motion that the Tennis League establish a division open to seniors enrolled in city and suburban county high schools. Those in favor of the motion, say *aye*.

SOME MEMBERS [Seated]: Aye!

(*continued on next page*)

Illustration: Voice, Standing, and Counted Vote (*continued*)

CHAIR: Those opposed, say *no*.

OTHER MEMBERS [Seated]: No!

CHAIR: The ayes have it, and the motion is carried. The Tennis League will . . .

MEMBER C [Seated]: Division!

CHAIR: A division is called for. Those in favor of the motion will rise.

SOME MEMBERS STAND

CHAIR: Be seated. Those opposed will rise.

OTHER MEMBERS STAND

CHAIR: Be seated. The affirmative has it, and the motion is adopted. The Tennis League will establish a division open to seniors enrolled in city and suburban county high schools. Is there further new business?

MEMBER C [Standing]: Madam President!

CHAIR: Member C.

MEMBER C: I move that the vote be counted. [Sits.]

ANOTHER MEMBER [Seated]: Second!

CHAIR: It is moved and seconded that the vote be counted. Those in favor of counting the vote, say *aye*.

SOME MEMBERS: Aye!

CHAIR: Those opposed, say *no*.

OTHER MEMBERS: No!

CHAIR: The ayes have it, and the motion is adopted. The vote will be counted. The question is on the adoption of the motion that the Tennis League establish a

---

(*continued on next page*)

Illustration: **Voice, Standing, and Counted Vote** (*continued*)

> division open to seniors enrolled in city and suburban
> county high schools. Those in favor of the motion will
> rise and remain standing until counted.
>
> SOME MEMBERS STAND [Chair counts, possibly assisted by
> secretary.]
>
> CHAIR: Be seated. Those opposed will rise and remain
> standing until counted.
>
> OTHER MEMBERS STAND [Chair counts, possibly assisted by
> secretary.]
>
> CHAIR: Be seated. There are 15 in the affirmative and 14 in
> the negative. The chair votes in the negative, making
> 15 in the affirmative and 15 in the negative, so that the
> negative has it and the motion is lost. Is there further
> new business?

4. Ballot Vote

Ballots are typically used in elections and may also be used for
other important decisions when there is a desire to keep secret how
each member votes. A motion may be made to conduct a ballot
vote. You may say, **"I move that the vote be taken by ballot."**

When a vote is to be by ballot, the presiding officer appoints
tellers (including a "Chairman of Tellers") to hand out, collect, and
count the ballots. Tellers are frequently chosen to represent all sides
of the issue at stake in the vote to be counted, and may vote themselves, as can the chair.

Before the tellers distribute the ballots, the chair instructs the
voters how to fold their ballots once they have marked them. In col-
lecting the ballots, the tellers have the responsibility of ensuring
that no member votes more than once.

When it appears that everyone has voted, the chair says, **"Have all voted who wish to do so?"** If there is no response, he or she continues, **"Since no one else wishes to vote,** [pause] **the polls are closed."** The tellers then count the ballots, usually in another room. The group often goes on to other business while awaiting the tellers' report.

The rules for counting ballots are described in detail in RONR (11th ed.), pages 415 to 417.

After counting, the tellers prepare a written report, in the form below.

Examples of Tellers' Reports

ELECTION
TELLERS' REPORT

Number of votes cast 97
Necessary for election (majority) . . . 49
Mr. Epstein received 51
Mrs. Wilson received 28
Mr. Rodriquez received 18

MOTION
TELLERS' REPORT

Number of votes cast 102
Necessary for adoption (majority) . . 52
Votes for motion 69
Votes against 33

The Chairman of Tellers seeks recognition, and when recognized, reads the report. The presiding officer then repeats the Tellers' Report (which is entered into the minutes) and officially announces who or what has won. If there is no majority (as may be the case when there are three or more candidates or alternatives), another ballot is taken. Individuals are never removed from candidacy on the next ballot unless they voluntarily withdraw. [RONR (11ᵗʰ ed.), pp. 417–19; 439–42.]

Example of Tellers' Report and Announcing Result

CHAIRMAN OF TELLERS [Stands]: Mr. President!

CHAIR: The Chairman of Tellers is recognized.

CHAIRMAN OF TELLERS: The Tellers' Report for the Office of Secretary is as follows.

> Number of votes cast: 35
> Necessary for election (majority): . . . 18
> Mr. Novak received: 22
> Mrs. Malloy received: . . . . 13 [Sits.]

CHAIR: The Tellers' Report for the Office of Secretary is as follows:

> Number of votes cast: 35
> Necessary for election(majority): . . . 18
> Mr. Novak received: 22
> Mrs. Malloy received: 13

Mr. Novak is elected Secretary.

---

5. Other Methods of Voting

Other methods of voting, such as roll-call and mail votes, are described in RONR (11ᵗʰ ed.) pages 419 to 429.

CHAPTER 9

NOMINATIONS AND ELECTIONS

CHAPTER CONTENTS

A. NOMINATIONS

A **nomination** is a formal proposal to the voting body, in an election to fill an office or position, suggesting a particular person as the one who should be elected. The usual practice is to have nominations, which tends to narrow the voting down to qualified and willing candidates. The two most common means of nominating candidates for office are nominations from the floor and by a nominating committee. Other methods are described in RONR (11th ed.) on page 431, lines 21–29, and on page 436, line 29 through page 438, line 16.

1. From the Floor

The chair calls for nominations from the floor by saying, for example, **"Nominations are now in order for the office of** President." Any member may then call out, for example, **"I nominate** Mrs. A," without first standing or being recognized by the chair. No seconds are necessary. The chair then announces, "Mrs. A **is nominated.**" When it appears that everyone who wishes to has made a nomination, the chair says, **"Are there any further nominations?** [Pause.] **If not,** [pause] **nominations are closed."** In the average society, a *motion* to *Close Nominations* is not a necessary part of the election procedure, and it should not generally be moved. [RONR (11th ed.), pp. 431–33, 435–36.]

2. By a Nominating Committee

When a nominating committee is to be used in an organized society, its members should be *elected*, not appointed. The committee may nominate one (or, less commonly, more than one) candidate for each office, and should secure each nominee's consent to serve before doing so. The Nominating Committee may report at the meeting at which the election is to be held or at a previous meeting, whichever procedure has been established by rule or custom. At that meeting, the chairman of the committee should report, **"Mr. President, the Nominating Committee submits the following nominations: For President**, Mrs. A; **for Vice President**, Mr. B [etc.]." The chair (that is, the assembly's presiding officer—not the chairman of the Nominating Committee) then calls for further nominations from the floor: **"For President,** Mrs. A **is nominated by the Nominating Committee. Are there further nominations for President?"** When there are no further nominations, the chair closes nominations as described earlier.

It is possible either to take nominations for all offices before electing any, or to take nominations for the first office, conduct the election for that office, and then repeat this procedure for each of the offices to be filled by election. [RONR (11th ed.), pp. 433–36.]

B. ELECTIONS

Elections are commonly conducted by ballot, under the procedure described in the previous chapter. If only one candidate has been nominated for an office, the chair simply declares the nominee elected (which is referred to as an election by "acclamation") *unless the organization's bylaws** require a ballot vote, in which case such a vote *must* be conducted. On any ballot, "write-in votes" may be cast for any eligible person even though he or she has not been nominated.

If no candidate receives a majority, balloting continues, retaining as candidates all who do not voluntarily withdraw.

An election becomes final when the chair announces the result if the candidate is present and does not decline or is absent but has previously consented to serve. Otherwise, it becomes final when an absent candidate is notified and does not immediately decline. If the

---

*Bylaws are explained in Chapter 10.

one elected declines, balloting continues until someone willing to accept receives a majority. If there is no different provision in the bylaws, a candidate takes office as soon as his or her election becomes final. Organizations often prefer to provide for new officers to assume office at the close of the meeting at which they are elected or at some later time. [RONR (11th ed.), pp. 439–42; p. 443, ll. 7–16; p. 444, ll. 17–32.]

Part IV

BYLAWS AND OTHER RULES
AND HOW TO USE THEM

CHAPTER

10

WHAT ARE THE BASIC TYPES OF RULES?

CHAPTER CONTENTS

A. THE RANKING ORDER OF RULES

A formal group with a continuing existence that makes decisions democratically at meetings needs rules dealing both with its own organization and purposes and with the procedure to be followed at its meetings.

Rules Governing an Assembly (from highest to lowest in authority)

1. **Law**: rules prescribed by applicable law
2. **Corporate charter**: for incorporated groups
3. **Bylaws or Constitution**: basic rules relating principally to itself as an organization
4. **Rules of order**: written rules of parliamentary procedure
   —**Special rules of order**: specific to organization
   —**Parliamentary authority**: general book of rules
5. **Standing rules**: administrative details
6. **Custom**

---

1. Law

If any federal, state, or local law governs the procedure of an organization (as is commonly true when a group is incorporated), that law supersedes any conflicting provision in any of the organization's rules. For example, under RONR a board can make decisions only in meetings, so that there is the possibility of debate and amendment before action is taken. [RONR (11th ed.), p. 486, l. 33 to p. 487, l. 9.] For groups incorporated in some states, however, the state corporation code authorizes decisions agreed to by every member of the board separately, without a board meeting being held. [RONR (11th ed.), p. 10, ll. 25–30.]

2. Corporate Charter

If and only if an organization is incorporated, the law of the state under which it is incorporated generally requires it to have a **corporate charter**. What this must contain, which varies from state to state, is established by law. [RONR (11th ed.), pp. 11–12.]

3. Bylaws or Constitution

In the majority of groups, the highest level of rules is contained in a document of the organization called the **bylaws**. Less commonly, organizations have a "constitution" instead of bylaws.* The bylaws contain the group's own basic rules relating principally to itself as an organization. They:

—describe the group's purpose;
—spell out the qualifications and method of selection of members;
—provide for officers, committees, and meetings (including the quorum); and
—may set up an executive board or board of directors.

Bylaws should include provisions for their own amendment that require previous notice of proposed amendments and at least a two-thirds vote for them to be adopted. Drafting and adopting bylaws is an essential step in forming a new organization. When adopting or amending bylaws, it is necessary to consult RONR (11th ed.), pages 565–99.

---

*Some organizations have both a constitution and bylaws (in which case the constitution outranks the bylaws). RONR (11th ed.), pp. 12–15, 565.

The activity of an organization must be conducted in compliance with its bylaws, and a main motion that violates them is not in order. [RONR (11th ed.), pp. 12–15; p. 111, ll. 4–6.]

4. Rules of Order

The regulation of the conduct of business in meetings is the function of **rules of order**. While bylaws must be written specifically for each different organization, in most respects rules for the conduct of meetings can be almost entirely the same from group to group. Indeed, people who belong to more than one group would find it very difficult if it were necessary to use a wholly different set of rules for the conduct of meetings for each group.

Normally, groups clearly identify the rules of order for their meetings by adopting in their bylaws the rules found in a well-established manual on the subject, which is then known as the organization's **parliamentary authority** (see p. 100). When the group finds a need to vary those rules for its own particular purposes, it then adopts **special rules of order** that supersede any conflicting rules in the book. (To take a common example, many groups adopt a special rule of order that sets tighter limits for debate, such as three minutes per speech rather than ten.)

Rules of order are intended to have stability from meeting to meeting. For this reason, to adopt or amend special rules of order requires previous notice *and* a two-thirds vote, or else—with or without previous notice—a vote of a majority of the entire membership of the voting body (not just of those who are present at the meeting).

A standard bylaw provision incorporating this approach reads, "The rules contained in the current edition of *Robert's Rules of Order Newly Revised* shall govern the Society in all cases to which they are applicable and in which they are not inconsistent with these bylaws and any special rules of order the Society may adopt."* [RONR (11th ed.), pp. 15–17; p. 580, ll. 6–24; p. 588, ll. 4–8.]

5. Standing Rules

Sometimes there are administrative details that are not important enough to be put in the bylaws and that do not relate to the conduct of business at meetings. For example, there might be a rule that the names of guests should be entered in a special guest register, and that they should be seated in a particular part of the meeting room. This sort of administrative detail is put into **standing rules**.

Standing rules require only a majority vote to adopt. To amend them takes either a majority vote with previous notice or, without notice, a two-thirds vote or a vote of a majority of the entire membership of the voting body. [RONR (11th ed.), p. 18.]

6. Custom

Sometimes, a group gets into the habit of doing something in the same way over and over again until it becomes an established **custom**. It comes to be followed practically as if it were a written rule.

No matter how long established a custom is, however, it can never conflict with a written rule—and if the conflict is pointed out, the written rule must be followed unless it is amended to incorporate the custom. For example, suppose it has been the regular practice in a particular group for the chair automatically to close debate whenever any member shouts, "I call the question." As Chapter 4 emphasizes, this violates the rule that allows debate to be ended, against the will of any member, only by a two-thirds vote (adopting

---

*The book you are now reading serves as an introduction and guide to *Robert's Rules of Order Newly Revised*, which, unlike this book, contains the complete rules of parliamentary procedure. This book is only a partial summary of that work, extensively cross-referenced to specific provisions in it. This book therefore is not itself suitable for adoption by any organization as its parliamentary authority. If any organization designates this book as its parliamentary authority, it actually adopts the current edition of *Robert's Rules of Order Newly Revised*.

the *Previous Question*)—and it is the rule, not the conflicting custom, which must be followed.

Even if there is no such conflict, the group itself may, by a majority vote, decide in any particular case not to follow a custom that has not been included in the organization's written rules. A custom that all officers are elected on one ballot, for example, could be changed in a particular election to have separate ballots for each office. [RONR (11th ed.), p. 19.]

B. MEMBERS' COPIES OF THE RULES

It is a good policy for every member to be given a booklet with the group's corporate charter (if any), bylaws, special rules of order, and standing rules. It is desirable to be familiar with these in order to participate fully in the group. [RONR (11th ed.), p. 14, l. 32 to p. 15, l. 3.]

11

HOW ARE RULES ENFORCED AND HOW ARE THEY SUSPENDED?

CHAPTER CONTENTS

A. POINT OF ORDER

The chair has the duty of making sure that the rules are followed. Any member may call the attention of the chair to a violation of the rules.

To do so, you stand up, interrupt the chair or a speaker if necessary, and without waiting to be recognized, call out, **"Point of order!"** Anyone speaking takes a seat, and the chair says, **"The member will state her point of order."** You then tell how you think the rules are being broken, and sit down.*

No second is necessary, and no vote is taken. Instead, the chair stands and rules on the point of order, saying, **"The Chair rules that the point of order is well taken"** or **"The Chair rules that the point of order is not well taken,"** briefly giving reasons (which are recorded in the minutes). [RONR (11th ed.), pp. 247–55.]

B. APPEAL

The group as a whole, not the chair, is the final authority in judging whether the rules have been violated. If you disagree with a ruling by the chair, you may *Appeal* it to the group as a whole.

Without waiting to be recognized, you stand and say, **"I appeal from the decision of the chair."** An appeal requires a second.

An appeal may generally be debated by the members, but unlike debate on other motions, each member may speak only once. The chair may speak in debate twice, the first time in preference over other members and the second time to close debate. How-

---

*With some important exceptions, a point of order must be timely. This means it must be made at the time the rules violation occurs. For example, suppose the chair states the question on a motion that has not been seconded. Once debate has already begun on that motion, it is too late to make the point of order that the motion had no second. RONR (11th ed.), pp. 250–51.

ever, the vote must be taken on the appeal without debate if the appeal:

a) relates to indecorum or a transgression of the rules of speaking;
b) relates to the priority of business; or
c) is made when an undebatable question is immediately pending or involved in the appeal.

An *Appeal* is stated and put to a vote as **"Shall the decision of the chair be sustained?"** It requires a majority vote in the *negative* to overturn the chair's ruling. A tie sustains the decision of the chair, and loses the appeal. [RONR (11th ed.), pp. 255–60.]

Point of Order and Appeal

CHAIR: The question is on the adoption of the motion: "That the Tennis League establish a division open to seniors enrolled in city and suburban county high schools." Are you ready for the question?

MEMBER A [Stands]: Madam President!

CHAIR: Mr. A.

MEMBER A: I move to add "comma, whose dues will be used for tennis scholarships." [Sits when finished.]

MEMBER B [Seated]: Second!

CHAIR: It is moved and seconded to add "comma, whose dues will be used for tennis scholarships." If the amendment is adopted, the main motion will read . . .

MEMBER C [Stands and interrupts]: Point of order!

CHAIR: The member will state her point of order.

MEMBER C: I make the point of order that under our rules, authorizing a new expenditure requires amending the

---

(continued on next page)

Point of Order and Appeal *(continued)*

---

budget. It cannot be done by amending this motion. [Sits when finished.]

CHAIR: The Chair rules that the point of order is well taken. A new expenditure does require an amendment of the budget. The amendment proposed to use the dues from students for tennis scholarships is therefore not in order. [This ruling will be included in the minutes.]

MEMBER A [Stands]: I appeal from the decision of the chair. [Sits.]

MEMBER B [Seated]: Second!

CHAIR: The decision of the chair is appealed from. The chair's ruling was that the amendment proposing to use the dues from students for tennis scholarships is not in order since under our Society's rules new expenditures may be authorized only by amending the budget, which we adopted at the annual meeting. The question is, "Shall the decision of the chair be sustained?" As the rules permit, the chair will speak first. Under our special rules of order, to protect the treasury and make the budgeting process meaningful, the only way to authorize spending money that is not already set forth in the budget is by amending the budget.

MEMBER A [Stands]: Madam President!

CHAIR: Mr. A.

MEMBER A: It is one thing to try to spend money already budgeted on something else. Then it makes sense to amend the budget. The new student division, however,

---

(continued on next page)

Point of Order and Appeal (*continued*)

> would bring in money that is over and above that in the budget, so we ought to be able to say what it will be used for without amending the budget. [Sits.]
>
> CHAIR: The chair intends to speak in rebuttal. Are there others who wish to speak first? [Pause for response.] The rule seems clear. It states that spending money not authorized by the budget requires an amendment to the budget, without making any exception when additional money is raised. The question is, "Shall the decision of the chair be sustained?" Those in favor of sustaining the chair's decision, say *aye*.
>
> SOME MEMBERS: Aye!
>
> CHAIR: Those opposed to sustaining this decision, say *no*.
>
> OTHER MEMBERS: No!
>
> CHAIR: The ayes have it and the decision of the chair is sustained. The question is now on the motion: "That the Tennis League establish a division open to seniors enrolled in city and suburban county high schools."

C. SUSPEND THE RULES

There are times when you wish to be able to do something forbidden by the rules. For example, you may want to allow a member to continue speaking when the allotted time has expired, or to permit consideration of a motion that would otherwise not be in order, or even to adopt a motion without debate or amendment.

In many cases like these the group may use the motion to *Suspend the Rules*, which requires a second, may be neither amended nor debated, and requires a two-thirds vote.

In moving to *Suspend the Rules*, you do not name the rule that is to be suspended. Instead you just describe what it is you want to be able to do that would violate the rules. For example, "I move to suspend the rules to give the speaker two more minutes," or "I move to suspend the rules which interfere with taking up the budget at this time." [RONR (11th ed.), pp. 260–67.]

Suspend the Rules

MEMBER A [Stands]: Madam President!

CHAIR: Mrs. A.

MEMBER A: I move to suspend the rules and allow the Membership Committee to report at this time. [Sits.]

MEMBER B [Seated]: Second!

CHAIR: It is moved and seconded to suspend the rules and allow the Membership Committee to report at this time. Those in favor of the motion will rise. . . . Be seated. Those opposed will rise. . . . Be seated. There are two thirds in the affirmative and the rules are suspended for the purpose of allowing the Membership Committee to report at this time.

D. PARLIAMENTARY INQUIRY

If you want to ask a question about the rules and how they apply to what is going on or to something you want to do, you may make a *Parliamentary Inquiry* of the chair.

If, and only if, your question requires immediate attention, you may interrupt a speaker to ask it. In any case, you do not have to be recognized first. You simply stand, and say, **"A parliamentary**

inquiry, please." The chair replies, **"The member will state the inquiry,"** and you say, for example, "Is it in order at this time to move to refer to a committee?" or "What is the pending question?"

The chair has the duty of responding to such questions when the answer may assist you to make an appropriate motion, raise a proper point of order, or understand the parliamentary situation or the effect of a motion.* However, the chair's answers are not rulings and consequently are not subject to appeal. If you believe the chair's response is wrong and want a chance to ask the full group to correct it, you must act contrary to the opinion expressed by the chair. Upon that action being ruled out of order, you may then appeal. [RONR (11th ed.), pp. 293–94.]

E. PARLIAMENTARIAN'S ROLE

To advise the presiding officer in responding to points of order and parliamentary inquiries, and generally to provide advice on conducting the meeting according to the rules, the president may appoint a **parliamentarian**. The parliamentarian, who should be seated next to the presiding officer, has a role that is purely advisory. Only the chair, not the parliamentarian, can rule on the proper application of the rules, and only on the most involved matters should the presiding officer ask the parliamentarian to give an explanation directly to the group. [RONR (11th ed.), pp. 465–67.]

---

*See RONR (11th ed.), p. 293, l. 32 to p. 294, l. 1. A *Request for Information* asks a question relevant to the business before the body but not related to parliamentary procedure, e.g., "How much uncommitted money is now in the treasury?" It is handled similarly to a *Parliamentary Inquiry*. It is *not* in order to raise a *Request for Information* to *give* information; instead, you must wait to be recognized and make your informative point as part of debate. RONR (11th ed.), pp. 294–95.

Part V

BEYOND THE BASICS

CHAPTER

12

LOOKING UP THE RULES: HOW TO USE *ROBERT'S RULES OF ORDER NEWLY REVISED*

CHAPTER CONTENTS

A. THE IMPORTANCE OF *ROBERT'S RULES OF ORDER NEWLY REVISED*

The book you are now reading is a simple overview and introduction to meeting rules. The rules themselves are contained in *Robert's Rules of Order Newly Revised* (abbreviated RONR), of which the eleventh is the current edition. If you are going to be involved in groups whose meetings are at all complex or deal with controversy, or if you are going to be an officer (*especially* the president) of *any* group, it is essential to go beyond this book and know how to look up the rules themselves in the rule book.

Robert's Rules of Order is America's foremost guide to parliamentary procedure. It is used by more organizations than any other parliamentary manual. *Robert's Rules of Order Newly Revised*, eleventh edition, published in 2011, supersedes all earlier editions as the parliamentary authority in organizations that have adopted *Robert's Rules of Order* in their bylaws.

Older editions have significant differences in the rules they contain and in page and section references. Because *Robert's Rules of Order* has been in use for so long, some of the earliest editions are no longer protected by copyright. They have therefore been republished and revised by different writers with varying qualifications in parliamentary law. Some have even been given titles like "modern edition" or "twenty-first century." None of these is the official, updated version.

It is important to get the right book. Other versions may be less expensive, but they will leave you looking in vain for a passage or a page that other group members have in front of them, and may not contain the rules that actually apply. Only the eleventh edition, with the title *Robert's Rules of Order Newly Revised*, is today's official rule book. It is readily available at most bookstores. You can also order the book online through the Robert's Rules Association website, www.robertsrules.com.

B. RONR AS A REFERENCE MANUAL

The RONR rule book is designed to provide an answer to nearly every question of parliamentary law that has so far been seen as possible to arise. At the same time, it is intended to convey an in-depth understanding of the subject overall, if read through. The resulting volume and detail may make reading the entire book seem daunting to many people. The average person may only occasionally be confronted with the small points that are necessarily dealt with if the book is to be fully useful. What you do need to know is how to locate, quickly, the rules that govern your particular situation somewhere in its 669 pages of text.

In short, it is important to understand how to use *Robert's Rules of Order Newly Revised* as a reference manual during and before meetings. For things covered in this brief book, references are included to exact pages in RONR so that you can easily find greater detail and the wording of the exact rules. However, because of this book's introductory nature, many important subjects are not even touched on here, and you need to know how to look up those as well. The purpose of this chapter, therefore, is to introduce you to the finding aids that will help you locate what you need in the rule book.

C. HOW RONR IS ORGANIZED

To begin, it is helpful to have a general idea of how *Robert's Rules of Order Newly Revised* is organized. The book has 20 chapters, and each chapter has one or more sections, numbered consecutively from the beginning of the book (63 sections in all).

1. Fundamentals

The first five chapters contain a treatment of fundamental concepts presented in an order chosen to minimize the need for referring to topics not yet explained. The first section of Chapter 1 includes a discussion of the nature of a "deliberative assembly" (the sort of group to which parliamentary rules of procedure apply) and its common types. The second section contains an explanation of the different kinds of rules an organization or assembly may adopt.

Chapter 2 contains a detailed but essentially elementary description of the basic procedures for conducting business in a meeting, assuming that no motions except main motions are introduced. In Chapter 3 the classification of motions and their order of precedence (see below) are explained. Chapter 4 describes the difference in meaning of "meeting" and "session" and their importance. It is placed at this point because these concepts frequently enter into all that follows. In Chapter 5 the main motion is thoroughly covered.

2. Motions

Chapters 6 through 9 contain the sections giving detailed coverage of each of the parliamentary motions. The sections covering the motions are constructed according to a uniform pattern that includes:

—a brief statement of the purpose of the motion;
—standard descriptive characteristics of the motion (see below);
—further rules and explanation; and
—form and example, in dialogue form whenever possible.

3. Body of Rules

Chapter 10 includes a full explanation of the renewal of motions, and also a brief section on dilatory and improper motions.

Chapters 11 through 16 all deal with the conduct of business at meetings, considered apart from the detailed study of specific motions.*

Chapter 17 deals with procedure at "mass meetings" and the organization of a permanent society.

Chapters 18, 19, and 20 cover bylaws, conventions, and disciplinary procedures.

4. Charts, Tables, and Lists

One part of RONR is especially useful for finding quick information about many important rules. On pages tinted gray at the outer edges, in the back of the book just before the index, are found charts, tables, and lists. To learn how to use them, it is useful first to understand a little about a matter not otherwise covered in this brief book—what to do when motions come into conflict—and the system RONR uses for classifying certain common rules for each motion—"standard descriptive characteristics."

D. USING RONR WHEN MOTIONS COME INTO CONFLICT

1. Taking Precedence and Yielding

As we have seen, only one main motion may be before the assembly for action, or be "pending," at a time. We have also seen,

---

*They cover quorum and order of business, assignment of the floor and debate, voting, nominations and elections, officers, minutes and officers' reports, and boards and committees.

however, that while a main motion is pending, certain motions that affect or interrupt consideration of the main motion may be moved. These are called **secondary motions**. Whichever motion, main or secondary, is directly before the group for action is called the **immediately pending** motion.

Suppose one motion—call it Motion A—is the immediately pending motion. It may be in order to move a secondary motion—Motion B—even though Motion A has not yet been disposed of. If that happens, Motion B temporarily displaces Motion A as the motion then directly before the group. In parliamentary terminology, Motion B becomes the immediately pending motion. If this is proper under the rules governing the two motions, we say that Motion B **takes precedence** over Motion A, and Motion A **yields** to Motion B.

For example, if a main motion is before the body, and someone offers an amendment, then the main motion yields to the amendment, which takes precedence over it and thus becomes the immediately pending motion.

Thus, one main and a number of secondary motions may be pending at one time, but only one motion can be immediately pending at any time. Any of the secondary motions described in this brief book can ordinarily be moved while a main motion is immediately pending, so a main motion normally yields to all secondary motions. [RONR (11th ed.), pp. 59–60.]

What happens, however, when a secondary motion is immediately pending, and a member wishes to move another secondary motion? Rules have been developed to answer this question.

2. The Order of Precedence of Motions

Many of the secondary motions so far considered, as well as others not previously described in this book, are *ranked* in an *Order of Precedence of Motions* that is given in Chart I on tinted page 4 in RONR. By consulting that chart, a simplified form of which is reproduced here, you can easily see that a higher-ranking motion on that list takes precedence over a motion listed lower than it on the list.

Thus, for example, the chart shows that the motion for the *Previous Question* can be moved while the motion to *Commit* is immediately pending, but the reverse is not true. Similarly, the motion for the *Previous Question* may not be moved while a motion to *Adjourn* is pending, since *Adjourn* is listed higher than *Previous Question*. [RONR (11th ed.), pp. 61–62.]

Order of Precedence of Motions

Fix the Time to Which to Adjourn*

Adjourn

Recess

Raise a Question of Privilege*

Call for the Orders of the Day* (To demand to take up the proper business in order)

Lay on the Table* (To interrupt the pending business so as to permit doing something else immediately)

Previous Question (Immediately to close debate and the making of certain motions)

Limit or Extend Limits of Debate

Postpone to a Certain Time

Commit

Amend

Postpone Indefinitely* (To drop the main motion without a direct vote on it)

Main Motion

Simplified from Chart I, RONR (11th ed.), tinted page 4.

---

*Motions marked with an asterisk have not been previously explained in this book but are summarized in Chapter 14.

3. Precedence of Incidental Motions

Other secondary motions previously considered in this brief book—namely, *Division of the Assembly, Motions Relating to Voting and the Polls, Point of Order, Appeal,* and *Suspend the Rules*—are not assigned positions in the Order of Precedence of Motions. Instead, these motions (along with others not described here) deal with questions of procedure arising out of another motion or item of business to which they are *incidental*. Motions falling into this subclass of secondary motions, called **incidental motions**, are applicable in their own types of special circumstances. They take precedence over any other motions that may be pending when those special circumstances occur. For example, a point of order takes precedence over any pending motion in the particular circumstance of a breach of the rules.

How may one use RONR to determine when particular incidental motions are or are not in order? The answer—and the answers to a number of other questions about particular motions—are found in RONR's coverage of each motion's standard descriptive characteristics.

E. STANDARD DESCRIPTIVE CHARACTERISTICS OF MOTIONS

Sections 11 through 37 of RONR contain detailed descriptions of particular motions, with a section for each motion. Toward the beginning of each of these sections are eight numbered **"standard descriptive characteristics"** (SDCs). By consulting numbers 1 and 2 of these for any motion, it is possible to determine the circumstances in which the motion is or is not in order: which motions it yields to or takes precedence over (# 1); and what motions or situations it applies to and which motions are applicable to it (# 2).

The other standard descriptive characteristics quickly provide other useful information about the particular motion. Having read to this point in this brief book, you should understand all of these:

3. Is it in order when another has the floor?
4. Does it require a second?
5. Is it debatable?
6. Is it amendable?
7. What vote is needed for its adoption?
8. Can it be reconsidered?

It will be helpful to glance through the sections on the individual motions (§11 through §37) to note how the standard descriptive characteristics and the rest of the text are arranged so that you will know where to find a detail when the occasion arises. [RONR (11th ed.), pp. 79–80.]

F. USING THE TABLES ON THE TINTED PAGES OF RONR

It is often not necessary to page through RONR to the section on a particular motion to find out the rules that are contained in the book's Standard Descriptive Characteristics (SDCs) 3–8. Instead, you may quickly look at Table II in the tinted pages. There, motions are listed alphabetically in rows and numbered individually for reference. There are columns for each of SDCs 3–8. Thus, it is possible to tell at a glance, for example, whether a particular motion may interrupt a speaker, or requires a two-thirds vote.

Another way to find much of the same information quickly is in Tables IV, V, VI, and VII. There, the information in SDCs 3–8 is arranged by rule; for example, Table IV contains alphabetical lists of motions that are in order when another has the floor and do not require a second, which are in order when another has the floor but must be seconded, and which are not in order when another has the floor but do not require a second.

Another useful feature is Table III, which contains a sample wording to be used when you are making each of the motions, with the motions again arranged in alphabetical order, with reference numbers exactly corresponding to those in Table II.

Table VIII summarizes the rules for counting election ballots and is particularly useful as a ready reference for tellers.

As described earlier in this chapter, for the thirteen ranking motions—those with a specific place in the Order of Precedence of Motions—Chart I gives, in diagram form, the elements of Standard Descriptive Characteristics 1 and 2.

G. TABLE OF CONTENTS AND INDEX

Carefully looking at RONR's table of contents, and frequently resorting to its index, should help you to find whatever else you need to know.

H. LEARNING MORE

Once you are familiar with the contents of this brief book, and know how to locate the rules in *Robert's Rules of Order Newly Revised*, you are ready to take the next step in increasing your mastery of meeting rules.

The first four chapters of RONR, totaling 99 pages, lay a comprehensive foundation for understanding virtually all of the basic concepts and fundamentals. Attentively reading those pages is the next logical step after going through this book.

After that, you may be guided by what most interests you or what you have the greatest need for: Look in the second half of RONR, after its coverage of the rules governing each specific motion, for detailed discussion of Quorum, Order of Business, Debate, Voting, Officers, Committees, and the like.

For Further Information on:	Read RONR Sections
Boards	49, 51
Bylaws, drawing up or amending	56, 57
Conventions	58, 59, 60
Committees	50, 51
Expelling or disciplining members	61, 63
Nominations & Elections	46; also 44, 45
Officers' duties	47
Organizing a new group	53, 54
Removing officers	62, 63

For further information, the Robert's Rules Association maintains a website, at www.robertsrules.com. On its "Question and Answer Forum" one may post queries and conduct discussion about any aspect of parliamentary procedure. The website also includes "RONR Official Interpretations" to deal with issues of parliamentary law arising between editions that RONR's authors deem useful to address.

CHAPTER

13

FREQUENTLY ASKED QUESTIONS

CHAPTER CONTENTS

CAUTION:

The answers given here to the questions presented are based upon the rules contained in this book and in *Robert's Rules of Order Newly Revised*. These rules are, in effect, *default* rules; that is to say, they govern only if there are no contrary provisions in any federal, state, or other law applicable to the society, or in the society's bylaws, or in any special rules of order that the society has adopted. This fact must always be kept in mind when reading any of the answers given.

The questions in this chapter are based on queries repeatedly received on the Question and Answer Forum maintained by the Robert's Rules Association at www.robertsrules.com.

Question 1:

Is it true that the president can vote only to break a tie?

Answer:

No, it is not true that the president can vote only to break a tie. If the president is a member of the voting body, he or she has exactly the same rights and privileges as all other members have, including the right to make motions, to speak in debate, and to vote on all questions. So, in meetings of a small board (where there are not more than about a dozen board members present), and in meetings of a committee, the presiding officer may exercise these rights and privileges as fully as any other member. However, the impartiality required of the presiding officer of any other type of assembly (especially a large one) precludes exercising the rights to make motions or speak in debate while presiding, and also requires refraining from voting except (i) when the vote is by ballot, or (ii) whenever his or her vote will affect the result.

When will the chair's vote affect the result? On a vote that is not by ballot, if a majority vote is required and there is a tie, he or she may vote in the affirmative to cause the motion to prevail. If there is one more in the affirmative than in the negative, the chair can create a tie by voting in the negative to cause the motion to fail. Similarly, if a two-thirds vote is required, he or she may vote either to cause, or to block, attainment of the necessary two thirds. [RONR (11th ed.), pp. 405–6; see also Table A, p. 190 of this book.]

Question 2:

Can ex-officio members vote, and are they counted in determining whether a quorum is present?

Answer:

"Ex officio" is a Latin term meaning "by virtue of office or position." Ex-officio members of boards and committees, therefore, are persons who are members by virtue of some other office or position that they hold. For example, if the bylaws of an organization provide for a Committee on Finance consisting of the treasurer and three other members appointed by the president, the treasurer is said to be an ex-officio member of the finance committee, since he or she is automatically a member of that committee by virtue of the fact that he or she holds the office of treasurer.

Without exception, ex-officio members of boards and committees have exactly the same rights and privileges as do all other members, including, of course, the right to vote. There are, however, two instances in which ex-officio members are not counted in determining the number required for a quorum or in determining whether or not a quorum is present. These two instances are:

1. In the case of the president, whenever the bylaws provide that the president shall be an ex-officio member of all committees (or of all committees with certain stated exceptions); and

2. When the ex-officio member of the board or committee is neither an ex-officio *officer* of the board or committee nor a

member, employee, or elected or appointed officer of the society (for example, when the governor of a state is made ex officio a member of a private college board).

Again, however, it should be emphasized that in these instances the ex-officio member still has all of the rights and privileges of membership, including the right to vote. [RONR (11th ed.), pp. 483–84; p. 497, ll. 20–29.]

Question 3:

Is it true that, once a quorum has been established, it continues to exist no matter how many members leave during the course of the meeting?

Answer:

No. Once a quorum at a meeting has been established, the continued presence of a quorum is presumed to exist only until the chair or any other member notices that a quorum is no longer present. If the chair notices the absence of a quorum, he or she should declare this fact, at least before taking any vote or stating the question on any new motion. Any member noticing the apparent absence of a quorum can and should make a *Point of Order* to that effect whenever another person is not speaking. It is dangerous to allow the transaction of substantive business to continue in the absence of a quorum. Although a *Point of Order* relating to the absence of a quorum is generally not permitted to affect prior action, if there is clear and convincing proof no quorum was present when business was transacted, the presiding officer can rule that business invalid (subject to appeal). [RONR (11th ed.), pp. 348–49; see also pp. 12–13 of this book.]

Question 4:

In determining the result of a vote, what constitutes a majority?

Answer:

The word "majority" in this context means, simply, *more than half*. The use of any other definition, such as 50 percent plus one, is apt to cause problems. Suppose in voting on a motion 17 votes are cast, 9 in favor and 8 opposed. Fifty percent of the votes cast is 8½ so that 50 percent plus one would be 9½. Under such an erroneous definition of a majority, one might say that the motion was not adopted because it did not receive 50 percent plus one of the votes cast, although it was, quite clearly, passed by a majority vote. [RONR (11ᵗʰ ed.), p. 400; see also p. 66 of this book.]

Question 5:

Can we round to the nearest number in computing the result of a vote? For example, since two thirds of 101 is 67.33 . . . , will 67 affirmative votes out of 101 votes cast meet the requirement of a two-thirds vote?

Answer:

No. The requirement of a two-thirds vote means *at least two thirds*. As a consequence, nothing less will do. If 101 votes are cast, 67 affirmative votes are not at least two thirds. They are less than two thirds, and will not suffice. [RONR (11ᵗʰ ed.), p. 401.]

Question 6:

Do abstention votes count?

Answer:

The phrase "abstention votes" is an oxymoron, an abstention being a refusal to vote. To abstain means to refrain from voting, and, as a consequence, there can be no such thing as an "abstention vote."

In the usual situation, where either a majority vote or a two-thirds vote is required, abstentions have absolutely no effect on the outcome of the vote since what is required is either a majority or two thirds of the votes cast. On the other hand, if the vote required is a majority or two thirds of the members *present*, or a majority or two thirds of the entire membership, an abstention will have the same effect as a "no" vote. Even in such a case, however, an abstention is not a vote and is not counted as a vote. [RONR (11th ed.), p. 400, ll. 7–12; p. 401, ll. 8–11; p. 403, ll. 13–24; see also p. 66 of this book.]

Question 7:
What is a vote of no confidence?

Answer:

The term "vote of no confidence" is not used or defined anywhere in RONR, and there is no mention of any motion for such a vote. However, this does not mean that an assembly cannot adopt a motion, if it wishes, expressing either its confidence or lack of confidence in any of its officers or subordinate boards or committees. Any such motion would simply be a main motion, and would have no effect other than to express the assembly's views concerning the matter. A vote of "no confidence" does not—as it would in the British Parliament—remove an officer from office.

Question 8:
How do you deal with a "friendly amendment"?

Answer:

On occasion, while a motion is being debated, someone will get up and offer what he or she terms a "friendly amendment" to the motion, the maker of the original motion will "accept" the amendment, and the chair will treat the motion as amended. This is wrong. Once a motion has been stated by the chair, it is no longer the property of the mover, but of the assembly. Any amendment, "friendly" or otherwise, must be adopted by the full body, either by a vote or by unanimous consent.

If it appears to the chair that an amendment (or any other motion) is uncontroversial, it is proper for the chair to ask if there is "any objection" to adopting the amendment. If no objection is made, the chair may declare the amendment adopted. If even one member objects, however, the amendment is subject to debate and vote like any other, regardless of whether its proposer calls it "friendly" and regardless of whether the maker of the original motion endorses its adoption. [RONR (11th ed.), p. 162.]

Question 9:

Isn't it true that a member who has a conflict of interest with respect to a motion cannot vote on the motion?

Answer:

Under the rules in RONR, no member can be compelled to refrain from voting simply because it is perceived that he or she may have some "conflict of interest" with respect to the motion under consideration. If a member has a direct personal or pecuniary (monetary) interest in a motion under consideration not common to other members, the rule in RONR is that he *should not* vote on such a motion, but even then he or she cannot be *compelled* to refrain from voting. [RONR (11th ed.), p. 407, ll. 21–31.]

Question 10:

Should proxy votes be counted?

Answer:

A "proxy" is a means by which a member who expects to be absent from a meeting authorizes someone else to act in his or her place at the meeting. Proxy voting is not permitted in ordinary deliberative assemblies unless federal, state, or other laws applicable to the society require it, or the bylaws of the organization authorize it, since proxy voting is incompatible with the essential characteristics of a deliberative assembly. As a consequence, the answers to any questions concerning the correct use of proxies, the extent of the power conferred by a proxy, the duration, revocability, or transferability of proxies, and so forth, must be found in the provisions of the law or bylaws which require or authorize their use. [RONR (11th ed.), pp. 428–29.]

Question 11:
Must debate on a motion stop immediately as soon as any member calls the question?

Answer:
It is a fairly common misconception that, after debate has continued for some time, if any member shouts out "Question!" or "I call the question!" debate must immediately cease and the chair must put the pending question to a vote. This is simply not the case. Any member who wishes to force an end to debate must first obtain the floor by being duly recognized to speak by the chair, and must then move the *Previous Question*. Such a motion must be seconded, and then adopted by a two-thirds vote, or by unanimous consent. It is not in order to interrupt a speaker with cries of "Question" or "Call the Question," and even if no one is speaking, it is still necessary to seek recognition. [RONR (11th ed.), p. 202; see also pp. 35–37 of this book.]

Question 12:
Isn't it always in order to move to table a motion to the next meeting?

Answer:
This question confuses the motion to *Lay on the Table* with the motion to *Postpone to a Certain Time* (the motion we discussed on pages 53–54). The purpose of the motion to *Lay on the Table* is to

enable an assembly, by majority vote and without debate, to lay a pending question aside temporarily when something else of immediate urgency has arisen or when something else needs to be addressed before consideration of the pending question is resumed. In ordinary societies it is rarely needed, and hence seldom in order. [RONR (11th ed.), pp. 209–18; see also p. 127 of this book.]

Question 13:
Can something be defeated by adopting a motion to table it?

Answer:
This is a common violation of fair procedure. Such a motion is not in order, because it would permit debate to be suppressed by a majority vote, and only a two-thirds vote can do that. The proper use of the motion to *Lay on the Table* is stated in the answer to Question 12, immediately above. [RONR (11th ed.), pp. 215–17.]

How *can* something be defeated without a direct vote on it?

Before debate on an original (ordinary substantive) main motion [see footnote on p. 129 of this book] has begun, you may raise an *Objection to Consideration of [the] Question*, which is undebatable and can suppress the main question by a two-thirds vote against consideration. [RONR (11th ed.), p. 216, l. 34 to p. 217, l. 2; pp. 267–70; see also p. 129 of this book.]

If debate on the main motion has begun and you want to get rid of that motion without a direct vote on it, use the motion to *Postpone Indefinitely*. That motion requires only a majority vote, but until it is adopted, it leaves the main question open to debate. [RONR (11th ed.), pp. 126–30; see also p. 126 of this book.]

If you feel that it is undesirable that debate take place, move the *Previous Question* immediately after moving to *Postpone Indefinitely*. If adopted by a two-thirds vote, this motion will cause an immediate vote on the motion to *Postpone Indefinitely* without further debate. [RONR (11th ed.), pp. 197–209.]

Question 14:

How can I get an item on the agenda for a meeting?

Answer:

For a proposed agenda to become the official agenda for a meeting, it must be adopted by the assembly at the outset of the meeting.

At the time that an agenda is presented for adoption, it is in order for any member to move to amend the proposed agenda by adding any item that the member desires to add, or by proposing any other change.

It is wrong to assume, as many do, that the president "sets the agenda." It is common for the president to prepare a proposed agenda, but that becomes binding only if it is adopted by the full assembly, perhaps after amendments as just described. [RONR (11th ed.), p. 372, ll. 24–35; see also p. 16 of this book.]

Question 15:

Isn't it necessary to summarize matters discussed at a meeting in the minutes of that meeting in order for the minutes to be complete?

Answer:

Not only is it not necessary to summarize matters discussed at a meeting in the minutes of that meeting, it is improper to do so. Minutes are a record of what was done at a meeting, not a record of what was said. [RONR (11th ed.), p. 468, ll. 16–18; see also p. 146 of this book.]

Question 16:

If minutes of a previous meeting are corrected, are the corrections entered in the minutes of the meeting at which the corrections were made?

Answer:

If corrections to minutes are made at the time when those minutes are originally submitted for approval, such corrections are made in the text of the minutes being approved. The minutes of the meeting at which the corrections are made should merely indicate that the minutes were approved "as corrected," without specifying what the correction was.

If it becomes necessary to correct minutes after they have initially been approved, such correction can be made by means of the motion to *Amend Something Previously Adopted*, which we discussed on pages 61–62. In this event, since the motion to *Amend Something Previously Adopted* is a main motion, the exact wording of that motion, whether adopted or rejected, should be entered in the minutes of the meeting at which it was considered. [RONR (11th ed.), p. 469, ll. 4–8; p. 475, ll. 18–24; see also p. 151 of this book.]

Question 17:
Can votes be taken in an executive session?

Answer:

Yes, votes can be taken in executive session. Proceedings in an executive session are secret, but are not restricted in any other way. [RONR (11th ed.), pp. 95–96.]

Question 18:
Is it possible to withdraw a resignation after it has been submitted?

Answer:

A resignation is a *Request to Be Excused from a Duty*, which is briefly described on page 131. It may be withdrawn in the same manner as any motion may be withdrawn—that is to say, before the proposed resignation has been placed before the assembly by the chair stating the question on its acceptance, it may be withdrawn without the consent of the assembly, but it may not be withdrawn without permission of the assembly once it has been placed before the assembly for its approval. [RONR (11th ed.), pp. 289–92; 295–97.]

Question 19:
Can we hold our board meetings by conference telephone call?

Answer:
You may hold board meetings by conference telephone call only if your bylaws specifically authorize you to do so. If they do, such meetings must be conducted in such a way that all members participating can hear each other at the same time, and rules should be adopted to specify the equipment required to participate, as well as methods for seeking recognition, obtaining the floor, submitting motions in writing, determining the presence of a quorum, and taking and verifying votes. [RONR (11th ed.), pp. 97–99; see also p. 159 of this book.]

It should be noted in this connection that the personal approval of a proposed action obtained from a majority of, or even all, board members separately is not valid board approval, since no meeting was held during which the proposed action could be properly debated. If action is taken by the board on the basis of individual approval, such action must be ratified by the board at a regular or properly called meeting of the board in order to become an official act. [RONR (11th ed.), p. 486, l. 33 to p. 487, l. 12.]

Question 20:
How can we get rid of officers we don't like before their term is up?

Answer:
It depends. If the bylaws just state a fixed term for the officer, such as "two years," or if they say the officer serves for a specified

term "*and* until [the officer's] successor is elected" (or words to that effect), then the group must use formal disciplinary proceedings, which involve the appointment of an investigating committee, preferral of charges, and the conduct of a formal trial. The procedure is complex and should be undertaken only after a careful review of Chapter XX of RONR.

On the other hand, if the bylaws state a term for the office but add "*or* until [the officer's] successor is elected," or contain other wording explicitly indicating that the officer may be removed before the term expires, then the officer can be removed from office by a two-thirds vote, by a majority vote when previous notice has been given, or by a vote of the majority of the entire membership—any one of which will suffice. A successor may thereafter be elected for the remainder of the term.

Of course, if the bylaws themselves establish a procedure for removal from office, that procedure must be followed. [RONR (11th ed.), pp. 653–54.]

CHAPTER

14

A SUMMARY OF MOTIONS

CHAPTER CONTENTS

A. INTRODUCTION

So far this book has focused on only those motions that are most commonly used. As a reference, however, this chapter will briefly describe not only these, but also most of the other motions normally used in parliamentary procedure, in terms of the type of situation in which each is of use. This will give you a "jumping off place" from which you can use the page references given here to locate their coverage in the eleventh edition of RONR, where you will find a fuller description of their use and the detailed rules that govern them.

B. MAIN MOTION

A **main motion** is a motion whose introduction brings business before the assembly. [RONR (11th ed.), pp. 100–125.]

C. SUBSIDIARY MOTIONS

Subsidiary motions assist the assembly in treating or disposing of a main motion (and sometimes other motions).

1) If an embarrassing main motion has been brought before the assembly, a member can propose to get rid of this question without bringing it to a direct vote, by moving to *Postpone Indefinitely*. [RONR (11th ed.), pp. 126–30.]

2) If a main motion might be more suitable or acceptable in an altered form, a proposal to change its wording (either to clarify or, within limits, to modify the meaning) before the main motion is voted on can be introduced by moving to *Amend*. [RONR (11th ed.), pp. 130–67.]

3) But it may be that much time would be required to amend the main motion properly, or that additional information is needed, so that it would be better to turn the motion or resolution over to a commit-

tee for study or redrafting before the assembly considers it further. Such action can be proposed by moving to **Commit** the main question—or **Refer** it to a committee. [RONR (11th ed.), pp. 168–79.]

4) If the assembly might prefer to consider the main motion later in the same meeting or at another meeting, this can be proposed by moving to **Postpone to a Certain Time**—also called the motion to **Postpone Definitely**, or simply to **Postpone**. [RONR (11th ed.), pp. 179–91.]

5) If it is desired to continue consideration of a motion but debate is consuming too much time, a member can move to place a limit on the debate. On the other hand, if special circumstances make it advisable to permit more or longer speeches than under the usual rules, a motion to do so can be made. Or, it may sometimes be desirable to combine the elements of limitation and extension, as in limiting the length of speeches but allowing more speeches per member. All such modifications of the normal limits of debate on a pending motion are proposed by means of the motion to **Limit or Extend Limits of Debate**. [RONR (11th ed.), pp. 191–97.]

6) If it is desired to close debate and amendment of a pending motion so that it will come to an immediate vote, this can be proposed by moving the **Previous Question**. [RONR (11th ed.), pp. 197–209.]

7) If there is reason for the assembly to lay the main motion aside temporarily without setting a time for resuming its consideration, but with the provision that it can be taken up again whenever a majority so decides, this can be proposed by the motion to **Lay on the Table**. [RONR (11th ed.), pp. 209–18.]

D. PRIVILEGED MOTIONS

Unlike subsidiary motions, **privileged motions** do not relate to the pending business, but have to do with special matters of immediate and overriding importance which, without debate, should be allowed to interrupt the consideration of anything else.

1) If the adopted program or order of business is not being followed, or if consideration of a question has been set for the present time and is now in order but the matter is not being taken
   up, a single member, by making a **Call for the Orders of the
   Day** [RONR (11th ed.), pp. 219–24], can require such a schedule to be
   enforced—unless the assembly decides by a two-thirds vote to
   set the orders of the day aside.

2) If a pressing situation is affecting a right or privilege of the assembly or of an individual member (for example, noise, inade-
   quate ventilation, introduction of a confidential subject in the
   presence of guests, etc.), a member can **Raise a Question of
   Privilege** [RONR (11th ed.), pp. 224–30], which permits him or her to
   interrupt pending business to state an urgent request or motion.
   If the matter is not simple enough to be taken care of informally, the chair then makes a ruling as to whether it is admitted
   as a question of privilege and whether it requires consideration
   before the pending business is resumed.

3) A short intermission in a meeting, even while business is pending, can be proposed by moving to **Recess** [RONR (11th ed.),
   pp. 230–33] for a specified length of time.

4) A member can propose to close the meeting entirely by moving
   to **Adjourn**. [RONR (11th ed.), pp. 233–42.] This motion can be made
   and the assembly can adjourn even while business is pending,
   provided that the time for the next meeting is established by a
   rule of the society or has been set by the assembly.

5) Under certain conditions while business is pending, the assembly—before adjourning or postponing the pending business—may
   wish to fix a date and hour, and sometimes the place, for another
   meeting, or (in an established society) for another meeting before
   the next regular meeting. In cases of this kind, the motion to **Fix
   the Time to Which to Adjourn** [RONR (11th ed.), pp. 242–46] can be
   made—even while a matter is pending—unless another meeting
   is already scheduled for later within the same session.

E. INCIDENTAL MOTIONS

Incidental motions relate, in different ways, to the pending business or to business otherwise at hand.

1) Although the presiding officer has the responsibility of enforcing the rules, any member who believes he or she has noticed a case where the chair is failing to do so can call attention to it by making a *Point of Order* [RONR (11th ed.), pp. 247–55] at the time the breach occurs. The effect is to require the chair to make a ruling on the question involved.

2) Although the duty of ruling on all questions of parliamentary procedure affecting the assembly's proceedings rests with the chair, any two members, by moving and seconding an *Appeal* [RONR (11th ed.), pp. 255–60] immediately after the chair has made such a ruling, can require him or her to submit the matter to a vote of the assembly.

3) When it is desired that the assembly take up a question or do something that would be in violation of a rule that applies, it can be proposed in some cases to *Suspend the Rules* [RONR (11th ed.), pp. 260–67] to permit accomplishment of the desired purpose.

4) If an original main motion* has been made and a member believes that it would do harm for the motion even to be discussed in the meeting, he or she can raise an *Objection to the Consideration of a Question* [RONR (11th ed.), pp. 267–70], provided he or she does so before consideration of the question has already begun; the assembly then votes on whether the main motion shall be considered (and if there is a two-thirds vote against consideration, the motion is dropped).

---

*Main motions actually fall into two subclasses, **original** main motions and **incidental** main motions (which are different from incidental motions). Original main motions are the ordinary substantive type we have discussed in this book. For an explanation of the two kinds of main motion, see RONR (11th ed.), pages 100–102.

5) If a pending main motion (or an amendment to it) contains two or more parts capable of standing as separate questions, the assembly can vote to treat each part individually in succession. Such a course is proposed by the motion for **Division of a Question**. [RONR (11th ed.), pp. 270–76.]

6) If the main motion is in the form of a resolution or document containing several paragraphs or sections which (although not separate questions) could be most efficiently handled by opening each paragraph or section to amendment one at a time (before the whole is finally voted on), such a procedure can be proposed by the motion for **Consideration by Paragraph or Seriatim**. [RONR (11th ed.), pp. 276–80.]

7) If a member doubts the accuracy of the chair's announcement of the result of a voice vote (or even a vote by show of hands)—or doubts that a representative number of persons voted—he can demand a **Division of the Assembly** [RONR (11th ed.), pp. 280–82]; a single member thus has the power to require a standing vote—but not to order a count, which only the chair or the assembly can do (see next item).

8) A member can move that a vote be taken (a) by ballot, (b) by roll call, or (c) by a counted standing vote, especially if a division of the assembly has appeared inconclusive and the chair neglects to order a count. This grouping also includes a motion (d) that the polls be closed or reopened in a ballot vote. All these motions are grouped under the heading of **Motions Relating to Methods of Voting and the Polls**. [RONR (11th ed.), pp. 283–86.]

9) If the bylaws or rules of the organization do not prescribe how nominations are to be made, and if the assembly has taken no action to do so prior to an election, any member can move while the election is pending (a) to specify one of various methods by which the candidates shall be nominated; or, if the need arises, (b) to close nominations, or (c) to reopen them; these are the **Motions Relating to Nominations**. [RONR (11th ed.), pp. 287–89.]

10) A member may **Request to Be Excused from a Duty** [RONR (11th ed.), pp. 289–92] if he or she wishes to be relieved from an obligation imposed upon him or her by the bylaws or by virtue of some position or office he or she holds.

11) There are several other types of **Requests and Inquiries** [RONR (11th ed.), pp. 292–99] which a member can make in connection with business that someone desires to introduce, or that is pending or has just been pending. These include:

   a) **Parliamentary Inquiry**—a request for the chair's opinion on a matter of parliamentary procedure as it relates to the business at hand—not involving a ruling. [RONR (11th ed.), pp. 293–94.]

   b) **Request for Information** (also called **Point of Information**)—an inquiry as to facts affecting the business at hand—directed to the chair or, through the chair, to a member. [RONR (11th ed.), pp. 294–95.]

   c) **Request for Permission (or Leave) to Withdraw or Modify a Motion** after it has been stated by the chair. [RONR (11th ed.), pp. 295–98.]

   d) **Request to Read Papers**. [RONR (11th ed.), pp. 298–99.]

   e) **Request for Any Other Privilege**. [RONR (11th ed.), p. 299.]

The first two types of inquiry are responded to by the chair, or by a member at the direction of the chair; the other requests can be granted only by the assembly.

F. MOTIONS THAT BRING A QUESTION AGAIN BEFORE THE ASSEMBLY

Motions That Bring a Question Again Before the Assembly, either by their adoption or by their introduction, enable the assembly for good reason to reopen a completed question during the same session, or to take up one that has been temporarily disposed of, or to change something previously adopted and still in force.

1) If it is desired to resume consideration of a main motion which lies on the table, it can be proposed by means of the motion to *Take from the Table* [RONR (11th ed.), pp. 300–304] that the motion or series become pending again.

2) If it is desired to cancel or countermand something that has been adopted and that has continuing force and effect, such action can be proposed by means of the motion to **Rescind** (or **Repeal**, or **Annul**); and by another form of the same parliamentary motion—that is, the motion to **Amend Something Previously Adopted**—it can be proposed to modify the wording or text previously adopted, or to substitute a different version. [RONR (11th ed.), pp. 305–10.]

3) If a question has been referred, or a task has been assigned, to a committee that has not yet made its final report and it is desired to take the matter out of the committee's hands, either so that the assembly itself can consider or act upon it or so that it can be dropped, such action can be proposed by means of the motion to **Discharge a Committee**. [RONR (11th ed.), pp. 310–15.]

4) If, in the same session that a motion has been voted on, but no later than the same day or the next day on which a business meeting is held, new information or a changed situation makes it appear that a different result might reflect the true will of the assembly, a member who voted with the prevailing side can, by moving to **Reconsider** [RONR (11th ed.), pp. 315–32] the vote, propose that the question shall come before the assembly again as if it had not previously been voted on.

Part VI

SO YOU'VE BEEN ELECTED (OR APPOINTED) . . .

CHAPTER

15

PRESIDENT OR VICE-PRESIDENT

CHAPTER CONTENTS

A. SIX STEPS TO EFFECTIVE PRESIDING

Making meetings orderly, fair, and expeditious largely depends on the knowledge and skill of the one who presides: the president or, in the president's absence, the vice-president.*

If you have been elected to one of these offices, or if you are thinking about becoming a candidate for it, how should you prepare to preside? Here are six steps to effective presiding.

1. Memorize Constantly Used Procedures

It is helpful to begin by mastering a few important, constantly used procedures, and memorizing the standard wordings for them. The foremost are those used in recognizing members to speak and in handling and voting (by voice or rising vote) on motions. They are described in Chapters 3 and 8, and the key wordings are available for ready reference in Table A, "Handling Motions as Chair," on pages 187–88. In particular, memorize the **bolded** wording beginning under "Stating the Motion" through that under "Rising Vote."

2. Make Sure All Know What's Being Debated and Voted On

One of your most important responsibilities is to make sure that the members always understand *exactly* what they are debating and voting on.

a) See That Motions Are Clearly Worded. The first necessity is to ensure that the wording of every motion is clear *before* you state it. Never state, uncorrected, a motion that the secretary would have

---

*For the method of selecting a temporary presiding officer when neither the president nor the vice-president is available, see RONR (11th ed.), pages 394–95, 452–53.

to paraphrase in order to put it into the minutes in understandable form. Instead, conduct a brief dialogue with the mover of the motion to see that it is put into suitable form, preserving its content to the mover's satisfaction.

Except with the simplest and clearest motions, take full advantage of your authority to require that the mover provide any main motion or amendment to you in writing. [RONR (11th ed.), p. 39, l. 33 to p. 40, l. 7.]

Depending on the circumstances, it may be useful to ask the group to "stand at ease" (see p. 17) while the mover writes down the motion and it is brought to you.

b) Repeat Wording of Motions Frequently. Develop the habit of repeating the wording of the motion as often as appropriate. When it is first introduced, you *state* it by saying, "**It is moved and seconded that** [repeating the exact words of the motion]." Whenever its consideration has been interrupted by other business, as well as whenever you feel some in the group may be unclear about it, say, "**The question is on the adoption of the motion that** [repeating the exact words of the motion as it then stands]."

c) Make the Effects of Amendments Clear. It is especially important to make sure everyone understands the effect of proposed amendments. When an amendment is first proposed, you should do three things:*

1) state the question as for any other motion: "It is moved and seconded to . . . ";
2) read the main motion (or the portion affected by the amendment) as it would stand if the amendment were adopted: "If the amendment is adopted, the main motion will read . . ."; and

---

*For the somewhat different approach in the case of an amendment in the form of a substitute, see pages 48–49 in this book.

3) make clear once more that it is the *amendment* that is under immediate consideration: "The question is on . . . ."

For example:

> CHAIR: [1] It is moved and seconded to strike out the words "establish a division open to" and insert the words "accept as members." [2] If the amendment is adopted, the main motion will read: "That the Tennis League accept as members seniors enrolled in city and suburban county high schools." [3] The question is on striking out the words "establish a division open to" and inserting the words "accept as members."

A similar three-step process should be followed when putting the amendment to a vote. If the amendment is lost, restate the main motion. If the amendment is adopted, then restate the motion as it has now been amended.

> CHAIR: [1] The question is on striking out the words "establish a division open to" and inserting the words "accept as members." [2] If the amendment is adopted, the motion will read: "That the Tennis League accept as members seniors enrolled in city and suburban county high schools." [3] Those in favor of striking out the words "establish a division open to" and inserting the words "accept as members," say *aye*. . . . Those opposed, say *no*. . . .
>
> The ayes have it and the amendment is adopted. The question is now on the main motion as amended,

(continued on next page)

(continued)

> "That the Tennis League accept as members seniors enrolled in city and suburban county high schools."
> OR
> The noes have it and the amendment is lost. The question is now on the main motion, "That the Tennis League establish a division open to seniors enrolled in city and suburban county high schools."

It is far better to risk taxing the patience of an assembly by repeating the wording of a motion on which all may be clear, than to risk taking a vote whose effect may be unclear to even a few members.

3. Learn How to Conduct Voting

Pay particular attention to learning the procedures and wording for the methods of voting by counted rising vote, show of hands, and counted show of hands. Learn the wording to be used when the chair's vote will affect the result. Most of these wordings are found in Chapter 8 and all are repeated for ready reference in Table A, "Handling Motions as Chair." If you do not memorize these forms (which is preferable), at least become familiar enough with them to be able to refer to them easily in Table A, beginning on page 188, so that you can use them without hesitation during a meeting.

4. Know the Steps in a Meeting

It is important to become familiar with the order of business, as explained in Chapter 2, and with the words used by the chair to call a meeting to order, handle the various steps in the order of business, and declare the meeting adjourned. These words are found in that chapter and repeated for ready reference in Table C, "Conducting a

Meeting as Chair," on page 193. Especially when you are first presiding, you may find it useful to have a copy of that page in front of you throughout the meeting.

You should STAND when:

a) calling a meeting to order or declaring it adjourned,
b) putting a question to a vote, and
c) ruling on a point of order or speaking during debate on an appeal.

You should SIT when a member is speaking in debate. In other circumstances, stand or sit as you find convenient in commanding the group's attention and preserving order. Be sure to arrange your position so that, whether standing or sitting, you can see and be seen by all those present at the meeting. [RONR (11th ed.), p. 22, ll. 9–12; p. 448, l. 29 to p. 449, l. 5; p. 451, ll. 8–28.]

5. Learn to Handle Points of Order and Appeals

Handling points of order and appeals, as described in Chapter 11 and repeated in Table A on page 191, should become second nature to you.

6. Know More About Parliamentary Procedure Than Other Members

With the core practice described in the first five steps mastered,* you should next make every effort to know more about par-

---

*If possible, repeatedly practice this core material in front of a mirror or with a small group of friends *before* first presiding. If the proper language and process of recognizing members, stating motions, putting motions to a vote (in the various ways possible), and handling amendments are so firmly embedded in your memory that you can comfortably use them almost unconsciously, at meetings you will be able to focus your attention on the content of the motions and proceedings, and on the other questions of parliamentary procedure sure to arise.

liamentary procedure than other members. At a minimum this means:

a) reading and re-reading this book (*RONR In Brief*) in its entirety;
b) having a copy of the current edition of *Robert's Rules of Order Newly Revised* (RONR), and becoming familiar with its arrangement and with the techniques for readily finding rules in it as described in Chapter 12 of this book; and
c) memorizing the chart entitled "Order of Precedence of Motions" on page 105 of this book.

Once you have done this, it is a very good idea to follow the suggestions in Chapter 12 for learning more in RONR.

B. MATERIALS YOU SHOULD HAVE AT MEETINGS

At each meeting, it is important that you have with you:

1) a copy of the group's bylaws and other rules;
2) a copy of the group's parliamentary authority, such as RONR;
3) a list of all committees and their members; and
4) a memorandum of the complete order of business for the meeting, ideally drawn up by or together with the secretary (see pp. 143–44).

CHAPTER

16

SECRETARY

CHAPTER CONTENTS

A. THE ROLE OF THE SECRETARY

As secretary, you have a number of important responsibilities before each meeting, during the meeting, in preparing minutes of the meeting, and outside of meetings.

B. SEND OUT THE "CALL" OR NOTICE OF MEETINGS

You send all members a "call" in advance of each meeting with information about its time, date, and location. [RONR (11th ed.), p. 459, ll. 18–19.]

Any member who wishes to give "previous notice" of a motion he or she intends to propose at the meeting may send the notice to you beforehand, and you must include it in the call at the group's expense. [RONR (11th ed.), p. 123, l. 35 to p. 124, l. 6.]

EXAMPLE OF CALL OF A MEETING

The regular monthly meeting of the Student Coalition will be held on Tuesday, January 11, 20__, at 8:30 P.M., in the Martyn Room of the University Center.

Ashley McClellan has given notice that at the meeting she will move to rescind the resolution adopted March 10, 20__, relating to student parking.

C. PREPARE ORDER OF BUSINESS FOR THE PRESIDING OFFICER

Before the meeting, based on the draft minutes from the last meeting, you should prepare a memorandum for the presiding officer that lists each item that is scheduled to come up, in proper order.

For example, if a committee was instructed to report, a particular motion was postponed to this meeting, and the previous meeting adjourned while another motion was still pending, your memorandum might look like this, in relevant part:*

Order of Business: Regular Meeting June 12, 20__

Invocation   8:30 P.M.
Pledge of Allegiance
Reading and Approval of Minutes
Reports
    Officers:
        President
        Vice-President
        Secretary
        Treasurer
    Board (by Secretary)
    Standing Committees:
        Membership Committee
        Program Committee
    Special Committee on New Headquarters (instructed
        to report)
Unfinished Business
    Motion "That the Coalition endorse new state taxes for
        education."
    Pending amendment "add 'other than property taxes.'"
    Motion postponed from last meeting: "That a committee
        be appointed to recruit Directors."**
New Business

---

*Reading Chapter 2 of this book will help you to make sense of this example. RONR (11th ed.), p. 459, ll. 24–28.

**This is actually an example of a "general order." General (and special) orders are described in RONR (11th ed.), pages 364–71.

D. DUTIES AT A MEETING

You should bring with you to every meeting:

a) the official membership roll;
b) a list of existing committees and their members;
c) the bylaws, special rules of order, and standing rules; and
d) recent minutes.

If both the president and vice-president are absent, it is your duty as secretary to call the meeting to order, and immediately to call for nominations and conduct an election of a temporary chairman.* [RONR (11th ed.), p. 453, ll. 3–16; p. 459, ll. 29–31.]

1. Read Minutes, Correspondence, and Resolutions to Meeting

Toward the beginning of the meeting, when directed by the chair, you read the minutes to the group. [See p. 14.] During officers' reports, when it comes time for the Secretary's Report, you read to the group any letters received. Throughout the meeting, you may be called upon to read to the group the text of motions, especially longer resolutions. [RONR (11th ed.), p. 33, ll. 18–34; p. 38, ll. 10–16.]

2. Record Motions

Both for the sake of the minutes and to assist the chair during the meeting, you *must* get down the *exact wording* of motions, especially main motions and amendments. You should not hesitate to ask the chair to have a motion repeated, or to ask the chair to exercise his or her authority to require that a main motion, an

---

*The method for conducting such an election may be that described in RONR (11th ed.), page 442, line 10 to page 443, line 16.

amendment, or instructions to a committee be put in writing. [RONR (11th ed.), p. 40, ll. 4–7.]

3. Assist with Voting

If a vote is counted, you may be called on to help the presiding officer do the count. [RONR (11th ed.), p. 51, l. 34 to p. 52, l. 1.]

If roll-call votes are ever used in your organization, you must become familiar with the procedure for conducting them, in which the secretary has the key role. (That procedure is described in RONR on pp. 420–22.)

E. PREPARE DRAFT MINUTES

The duty people most commonly think of in connection with the secretary is drafting the minutes, or official record, of each meeting. Frequently, secretaries make unneeded work for themselves by putting far more into the minutes than is required or appropriate. The most frequent mistakes are trying to summarize the reports offered and arguments made in debate, and including all of the amendments and other secondary motions. In fact, in standard form the minutes should generally include only what was *done*, not what was *said*. [RONR (11th ed.), p. 468, ll. 16–18.]

They should include the text of main motions as they stood when finally voted on. With a couple of exceptions (to be described shortly), they should not include the text of secondary motions.*

The form for standard minutes is divided into four parts: the first paragraph, the body, the last paragraph, and the signature.

---

*The use of a tape recorder by the secretary can be helpful in preparing the minutes, but a transcription from it should never be used as the minutes themselves.

1. First Paragraph

The first paragraph of the minutes should include:

1) kind of meeting (e.g., regular or special);
2) name of organization or assembly;
3) date, time, and (unless always the same) place;
4) presence of president and secretary or names of their substitutes; and
5) whether minutes of previous meeting(s) were read and approved, or "approved as corrected." The corrections themselves should be made in the minutes *being* corrected, and not further described in the minutes of the meeting *at which* they are corrected.

Example of First Paragraph of Minutes

The regular monthly meeting of the Student Coalition was held on Tuesday, January 11, 20__, at 8:30 P.M., in the Martyn Room of the University Center, the President being in the chair and the Secretary being present. The minutes of the last meeting were read and approved as corrected.

---

2. Body of Minutes

The body of the minutes should have a separate paragraph for each subject matter. It should never include the secretary's opinion on anything said or done (for example, do *not* write, "X gave an excellent report on . . . ."). The name and subject of a guest speaker or other program may be given, but no summary of the talk.

a) Reports. The minutes do not include the contents of the reports of officers or committees, except as may be necessary to cover motions arising out of them. An example of how the minutes should describe reports without motions is: "Reports were given by President

Darian Will, Vice-President Roxana Arthur, Secretary Jolan Davis, Treasurer Jose Rhinehart, and Karen Wilson, Chairman, on behalf of the Education Committee." An example of how the minutes should treat a report with a motion is: "Dennis McAuliffe, reporting on behalf of the Membership Committee, moved 'that Stacie Johnson be admitted to membership in the Society.'"

b) Main Motions Only. All main motions which are moved during the course of a meeting (excepting *only* those which are withdrawn by the maker) should be recorded in the minutes. With the two exceptions about to be discussed, the minutes should contain the text only of *main* motions, whether adopted or defeated. In the case of all main motions, the name of the mover—but *not* the seconder—should be given.

The text of each main motion should be recorded in the minutes, using the wording of the motion immediately before it was finally voted on or otherwise disposed of. This wording will incorporate any amendments that were adopted during the main motion's consideration. The minutes should say whether the motion was adopted or lost "after debate," "after amendment," or "after debate and amendment." In the normal case of a main motion that was finally voted on or otherwise disposed of at the meeting, *the minutes should not include any further information about proposed amendments, whether or not they were adopted.*

Examples of Minutes' Treatment of Motions

Dennis McAuliffe moved "that Stacie Johnson be admitted to membership." The motion was adopted after debate.

Sam Lee moved adoption of a resolution which, after debate and amendment, was adopted as follows: "*Resolved,* That the Coalition support the establishment of publicly financed health clinics in public elementary and secondary schools so long as such clinics obtain parental consent to treat students."

c) Exception: Secondary Motions When Main Motion Carried Over to Another Meeting. The first of the two exceptional cases in which amendments or other secondary motions are separately reported in the minutes occurs when a main motion is carried over to a later meeting. Then the minutes include the main motion as it stood at the time, together with any pending amendments or other secondary motions carried over with it, as well as the motion that caused it to be carried over. For example:

> Dahlia Sutherland moved "that the Coalition support the establishment of a summer camp for children on its lakefront property." Lewis Thomas moved to amend this motion by inserting the words "inner-city" before "children." On motion of Angela Mercouri, the motion to establish the camp, with the pending amendment, was referred to a committee of three to be appointed by the chair with instructions to report at the next meeting.

d) Exception: Secondary Motions Needed for Clarity. The second exception occurs when it is necessary to make reference to a secondary motion for clarity and completeness, such as "a ballot vote having been ordered, the tellers reported . . . ."

e) Votes, Notices of Motions, Points of Order, and Appeals. Other items that should be in the body of the minutes are these:

- *Votes:*
  —Usually, only *that* a motion was "adopted" or "lost";
  —If a count or ballot vote was ordered, the number of votes on each side;
  —For roll-call votes, the names of those voting on each side and of those answering "Present" [RONR (11th ed.), p. 470, ll. 29–33.];

- Content of any *notices of motions* given to provide "previous no-tice" that the motions will be considered at the next meeting; and
- *Points of Order* and *Appeals*, whether sustained or lost, together with the reasons given by the chair for his or her ruling. [RONR (11th ed.), p. 470, ll. 14–17.]

3. Last paragraph

The last paragraph should give the time of adjournment but need not list the mover or fact of adoption of any motion to *Adjourn*. It should read simply, for example, "The meeting adjourned at 7:18 P.M."

4. Signature

The minutes should be signed by the secretary and, if the group wishes, the president. There is no need to include, "Respectfully submitted."

A helpful sample set of minutes is found on pages 472–73 of RONR, and it is advisable for any newly elected secretary to review, and later refer to, the more detailed treatment of minutes in that book. [RONR (11th ed.), pp. 468–76.]

F. CORRECTION AND APPROVAL OF MINUTES

It is important to recognize that the minutes you draft are only *proposed* minutes, which do not become the official record of pro-ceedings until approved, perhaps with corrections, by the organiza-tion. Often the secretary will send copies of the draft minutes out in advance of the meeting at which they are to be approved, typically with the call, but it is advisable to label them "draft" to help members to remember that they may yet be corrected before being approved.

Any corrections made to the draft minutes at the meeting at which they are approved are made in the text of the minutes being approved. The minutes of the meeting at which the corrections are made should merely indicate that the minutes were approved "as corrected," without specifying the corrections. [RONR (11th ed.), p. 469, ll. 4–8; see also q. 16 on pp. 120–21 of this book.]

G. DUTIES OUTSIDE MEETING

It is your job to keep the official records of the group. These include the bylaws, special rules of order and standing rules, minutes, membership roll, and committee reports. You must make the minutes available for inspection by the members at reasonable times and places, and provide committees with any documents necessary for their work.

It is also your responsibility to conduct the group's official correspondence, including officially notifying officers, committee members, and convention delegates of their election or appointment.

As secretary, you may also need to certify with your signature acts of the organization, and sometimes the credentials of delegates representing the group at a convention. [RONR (11th ed.), pp. 458–60.]

17

TREASURER

CHAPTER CONTENTS

A. DUTIES

As treasurer, you are the officer entrusted with custody of the organization's funds, which you spend only by authority of the society or as the bylaws provide. In many organizations, it is also your responsibility to bill and collect dues from members. [RONR (11ᵗʰ ed.), p. 461.]

B. TREASURER'S REPORT

At each meeting, the chair may ask for a "Treasurer's Report," which may consist of your oral statement of the cash balance on hand, or of this balance less outstanding obligations. No vote or other action is taken by the group on this sort of treasurer's report.

Annually, however, you must submit a full financial report, dated as of December 31 (unless the organization has a different "fiscal year," in which case it is dated as of the last day of the fiscal year). For a small group with simple financial affairs primarily involving cash, a suitable form is illustrated on the next page. Of course, many other organizations use more complex bookkeeping systems, and then the sort of report submitted should be in accord with standard accounting procedures.

This annual report is referred to auditors, and the auditors' report is submitted to the assembly for a vote of approval. An unaudited treasurer's report is itself never directly subject to action by the assembly, except to be referred to the auditors. [RONR (11ᵗʰ ed.), pp. 477–79.]

Report of the Treasurer
Of the L.M. Society for the Year
Ending December 31, 20__

Balance on hand January 1, 20__		$1,253.25
Receipts		
Members' Dues	$630.00	
Proceeds from Spring Barbecue	296.75	
Fines	12.00	
Total Receipts		938.75
Total		$2,192.00
Disbursements		
Rent of Hall	$500.00	
Custodial Service Fees	175.00	
Stationery and Printing	122.40	
Postage	84.00	
Total Disbursements		$ 881.40
Balance on hand December 31, 20__		1,310.60
Total		$2,192.00

Richard Larson, Treasurer

Audited and found correct
  Colleen Burke
  Randolph Schuler
    Auditing Committee

C. AUDITS

In many organizations, audits are done by independent certified public accountants (CPAs). An audit is an examination and verification of the treasurer's accounts and financial statements. In those whose size or nature does not justify the expense of audit by CPAs, an auditing committee of two or more members is created to examine the financial accounts and certify whether the treasurer's report based upon them is correct. This may either be a standing committee or a special committee created each year.

It is preferable to provide your annual report to the auditors for them to complete their review before the annual or other meeting at which you give it to the assembly. In that case, if they find no irregularities, it is endorsed "Audited and found correct" with the names of the members of the auditing committee, and you read out this certification as you conclude your presentation. The chair then immediately states the question on adopting the auditors' report. Its approval by the assembly relieves you of responsibility for the period covered by the report, except in case of fraud.

If, instead, you present an unaudited annual report, the chair, without waiting for a motion, says, **"The report is referred to the Auditing Committee** [or **"to the auditors"**]**."** If no auditing committee or auditors have been previously selected, however, the assembly then adopts a motion to refer the report to an auditing committee, specifying how it is to be appointed. When the committee has finished its work, its chairman submits the committee report to the assembly, which then votes whether or not to approve it. [RONR (11th ed.), pp. 479–80.]

BOARD MEMBER

CHAPTER CONTENTS

A. INDEPENDENT BOARDS

A board may itself be the highest governing authority of an organization or corporation. This may be true of the board of an organization that has no voting membership other than the board members, such as a foundation or university. It may also apply to an entity, such as a stock corporation, in which the voting members (for example, stockholders) elect members of the board but otherwise exercise almost no binding authority over the affairs of the organization. This type of board can adopt its own rules. [RONR (11th ed.), p. 483, ll. 13–16; p. 484, ll. 14–22; p. 486, ll. 25–28.]

B. SUBORDINATE BOARDS

On the other hand, a board may be part of an organization with an assembly of voting members, to which the board is subordinate. In this case the assembly elects the board members, often at the same meeting at which it elects officers. This type of board is given varying degrees of authority to act for the group between meetings of that assembly, but generally must follow the assembly's instructions. It can adopt its own rules as long as they do not conflict with the bylaws, parliamentary authority, or other rules of the organization. [RONR (11th ed.), p. 482, l. 25 to p. 483, l. 13; p. 486, ll. 13–19.]

C. EXECUTIVE COMMITTEE

When a board is large or its members widely spread geographically, there may also be an executive committee, often made up of the officers. An executive committee is a "board within a board" that is normally empowered to act in the board's place between board meetings, subject to the board's instructions. [RONR (11th ed.), p. 485.]

D. PROCEDURE IN BOARDS

As a board member, what you need to know to participate properly in board meetings depends on their size. If there are more than about a dozen board members at a meeting, the same procedures are followed as at other meetings, exactly as described in the rest of this book.

If, however, not more than about a dozen board members are present, a more informal procedure is followed [RONR (11th ed.), pp. 487–88.]:

Informal Procedure in Small Boards

+ Board members may raise a hand instead of standing when seeking to obtain the floor, and may remain seated while making motions or speaking.
+ Motions need not be seconded.
+ A board member may speak any number of times (not just twice) on a debatable question, except that the regular rules apply to appeals (see p. 90).
+ A motion does not have to be pending in order to discuss a subject informally.
+ Votes can be taken initially by a show of hands.
+ If a proposal is perfectly clear to everyone, it may be voted on even though no formal motion has been made.
+ In putting questions to a vote, the chairman need not stand.
+ If the chairman is a member of the board, he or she can, without giving up the chair, participate in debate, make motions, and vote on all questions.

E. VALIDITY OF BOARD ACTION

In order for the actions of a board to be valid, they must be agreed to by a majority vote at a regular or properly called meeting of the board of which every board member has been notified. A quorum—a majority of the board members in office, if no different number is set by the bylaws—must be present. [RONR (11th ed.), p. 486, l. 33 to p. 487, l. 9; see also q. 19 on p. 122 of this book.]

If the bylaws authorize the board to do so, however, it may also meet by videoconference or teleconference (including over the Internet) so long as all persons participating can hear each other at the same time (and, if by a videoconference, can see each other as well).*

---

*RONR (11th ed.), pp. 97–99. "Polling" or consultation with each member of the board separately is not an acceptable substitute, because it does not allow an opportunity for members to participate in and be influenced by debate before voting. RONR (11th ed.), p. 487, ll. 4–9; p. 503, ll. 21–24.

19

COMMITTEE CHAIRMAN OR MEMBER

CHAPTER CONTENTS

A. THE IMPORTANCE OF COMMITTEES

A great deal of the work of many organizations is done in committees, so your position as a member of a committee—and especially your position if you are a committee chairman—is an important one.

B. SCHEDULING COMMITTEE MEETINGS

The first meeting of a committee is scheduled, or *called*, by the chairman giving notice of it to all the committee members. If the chairman fails to call a meeting, any two members can do so. To schedule subsequent meetings, the committee can vote to adjourn to a later time. Alternatively, the committee can just adjourn, in which case it meets again at the call of the chairman. [RONR (11th ed.), p. 499, l. 19 to p. 500, l. 2; p. 501, l. 28 to p. 502, l. 11.]

C. VALIDITY OF COMMITTEE ACTION

As with a board, a committee acts validly if its decisions are agreed to by a majority vote at a properly called meeting of which every committee member was notified and at which a quorum—a majority of its members—is present. If properly authorized, meetings may be by videoconference or teleconference (including over the Internet) so long as all persons participating can hear each other at the same time (and, if a videoconference, can see each other as well).

Unlike a board, however, a committee may also validly act without a meeting if what it decides is agreed to by every one of its members. [RONR (11th ed.), pp. 97–99; p. 503, ll. 14–28.]

D. COMMITTEE PROCEDURE

Only committee members have the right to be present during its actual deliberations. When the committee will be making substantive recommendations or decisions on an important matter, however, it should schedule a **hearing** at which any member of the organization can appear before it to present views on the subject.

While the chairman usually acts as secretary in small committees, in many committees another member is elected as secretary to prepare temporary memoranda for the committee's use, somewhat like minutes of the committee meetings. These, however, are not approved or corrected at the next meeting or permanently retained, as are the minutes of an assembly.

During committee meetings, unlike meetings of the organization's full membership, the chairman has the right to make and debate motions; indeed, he or she is usually the most active participant in the discussion and work of the committee. Motions to close or limit debate are not allowed. In other respects, committees use the informal procedure for boards of about a dozen or fewer members described in the previous chapter. This informal procedure is followed in a committee even if the committee's membership exceeds a dozen, unless it is otherwise instructed by its parent assembly.

A committee can take it upon itself to appoint subcommittees of its own members, which report to it. Unless authorized by the assembly, however, it cannot adopt rules of its own. [RONR (11th ed.), p. 497, ll. 14–19; pp. 499–501.]

E. STANDING AND SPECIAL COMMITTEES

As described in Chapter 6, there are two types of committees: **standing committees**, which have a continuing existence and function, normally responsibility for a particular subject matter (for example, the Membership Committee), and **special (ad hoc, or select) committees**, which are created for a particular purpose and go out of existence when that purpose is completed. Usually, members of standing committees are either elected at the same time as the officers or appointed by the president at the beginning of his or her term. Members of special committees are selected when the committees are created, as described in Chapter 6. [RONR (11th ed.), p. 490, l. 32 to p. 496, l. 35.]

New committees may not be established by the president unless the bylaws expressly grant this power. Although the president may, in his or her report, recommend that a special committee be constituted, only the assembly may create it. If the bylaws empower the president to "appoint all committees (except the Nominating Committee)," that gives him or her the authority to appoint the *members* of committees, but not to create new ones. [RONR (11th ed.), p. 495, l. 29 to p. 496, l. 1.]

A standing committee can originate recommendations and motions concerning subjects within its area of responsibility, without specific instructions from the assembly. If a special committee is created with instructions to deal with a specified subject (as distinct from a particular motion), it can originate recommendations and motions concerning that subject. In addition, either type of committee may have particular motions referred to it by the assembly for consideration, in which case the committee normally reports the referred motions back to the assembly with its recommendations.

F. COMMITTEE REPORTS

Whether a committee originates a motion or considers a motion referred to it by the assembly, the committee conveys its views to the assembly by means of a *report*. Often it is best for the formal committee report to be confined as much as possible to the committee's recommendations, in the form of proposed resolutions or otherwise. The person who presents the report can then add brief oral explanations of supporting reasons. If a more detailed report is considered necessary, it can include:

1) a description of the way in which the committee undertook its charge;
2) the facts uncovered or information obtained;
3) the committee's findings or conclusions; and
4) resolutions or recommendations. [RONR (11th ed.), pp. 503–6.]

The committee chairman presents the report unless he or she declines, in which case the committee designates another of its members to do so.

When assigned the floor (normally at the time for committee reports in the order of business), the chairman or other reporting member either gives the report orally or, if it is written, reads it or gives it to the secretary to read. At the conclusion of the report, the chairman or other reporting member makes any necessary motion to implement the report's recommendations, for example: **"By direction of the committee, I move the adoption of the resolution just read."*** Assuming the committee has at least two members, no second is required. [RONR (11th ed.), pp. 506–8; pp. 514–29.]

---

*For the procedure when a committee recommends new amendments to a motion that has been referred to it, see RONR (11th ed.), pp. 520–25.

SAMPLE COMMITTEE REPORTS

Committee Originating Resolution

The Buildings and Grounds Committee wishes to report that the clubhouse roof was extensively damaged by the hurricane last week. The committee therefore recommends the adoption of the following resolution: "*Resolved*, That the Buildings and Grounds Committee be authorized to request bids for repair of the clubhouse roof and to award a contract for the same, provided that, without further authorization, the cost shall not exceed $5,000."

George Wilson, Chairman

Madam President, by direction of the committee, I move the adoption of the resolution just read.

Committee Reporting on Referred Resolution

The committee to which was referred the resolution, "*Resolved*, That the proceeds from the recent bequest to the Association from the Asquith estate be invested in stock of the Consolidated Development Corporation," recommends that, for the resolution, the following substitute be adopted, "*Resolved*, That the Executive Board be authorized to retain reputable investment counsel with a view to determining appropriate investment of the proceeds from the Asquith bequest."

Judith Sarner, Chairman

Mr. President, on behalf of the committee, I move that the resolution last read be substituted for the referred resolution.

CONVENTION DELEGATE OR ALTERNATE

CHAPTER CONTENTS

A. THE NATURE OF A
CONVENTION

A **convention** is an assembly of delegates. **Delegates** are representatives of the constituent units of a larger group. For example, a national organization with hundreds or thousands of chapters might hold an annual convention, composed of delegates separately elected by each chapter, for the purpose of electing national officers and setting policies for the organization as a whole. The convention serves as a single deliberative body acting in the name of the entire organization. [RONR (11th ed.), p. 600, ll. 3–9.]

The information in this chapter is intended primarily for the guidance of the member of a local branch of a state or national organization who may be elected as a convention delegate or alternate. If you share responsibility for planning or conducting a convention, if you are to preside at a convention, or if you are a member (especially the chair) of any of the convention committees, it is essential for you also to read the much more extensive coverage of conventions in RONR, eleventh edition, pages 600–640.

B. THE RIGHTS AND DUTIES OF A
DELEGATE

The procedures for determining the number and qualifications of delegates, and how they are selected, are spelled out in your organization's bylaws. Your unit must send in "credentials" forms designating the unit's delegates (and alternates; see next section) before a date, specified by the bylaws, in advance of the convention.

When you are selected as a delegate to a convention, you have the duty of attending the business meetings at the convention. After arriving at the convention site, you go to the credentials desk to register and receive a badge or other insignia to identify you as a delegate. This initially entitles you to take your place in the convention hall.

You are free to vote as you see fit on matters that come before the convention, except that you must vote in accordance with any instructions your unit may have chosen, by majority vote, to give you. After returning, it is your duty to be prepared to present to the unit for which you are a delegate an information report on what happened. [RONR (11th ed.), pp. 601–3; p. 612, ll. 6–18; p. 605, ll. 18–29.]

C. ALTERNATES AND HOW THEY REPLACE DELEGATES

Usually **alternates** are selected in a number equal to the number of delegates, under procedures set out in the bylaws. When you are selected as an alternate, your job is to be available in case a delegate is unable to fulfill his or her duties. Like those selected as delegates, after arrival at the convention site you go to the credentials desk to register and receive a badge or other insignia. This identifies you as an alternate and gives you access to the alternates' section of the convention hall.

Unless each alternate is paired with a specific delegate to replace, alternates fill vacancies in the **delegation**—the group of delegates representing a particular unit—in the order in which they were elected. (When the president of a unit serves as a delegate by virtue of that office, then the vice-president is the alternate for the president.)

If a delegate fails to register at the convention, the appropriate alternate is registered as a delegate in his or her place. If a delegate has already registered at the convention, then an alternate may replace that delegate only when the Credentials Committee is presented with proper evidence of the delegate's withdrawal and re-registers the alternate as the new delegate. *A delegate's temporary absence from the convention hall does not entitle an alternate to vote, speak, or make motions in the delegate's place, even with the delegate's authorization.* [RONR (11th ed.), pp. 604–5.]

D. HOW A CONVENTION DIFFERS FROM OTHER MEETINGS

Although there are many similarities in the way business is conducted at a convention and the way it is conducted at other meetings, there are also significant differences. It is important for you to become familiar with the most important of these differences in order to be an effective delegate or alternate.

Because each convention is normally composed of a new set of delegates, it must begin with a series of steps by which it "organizes" itself before it can go on to consider substantive business. How a convention organizes itself can have a great impact on the decisions it ultimately makes, so it is very important for you as a delegate or alternate to understand these procedures and how you can affect them.

E. THE THREE IMPORTANT STEPS IN BEGINNING A CONVENTION

After any opening ceremonies (which may include an invocation, reciting the Pledge of Allegiance, speeches by dignitaries, and the like), a convention organizes itself through three steps:

1) establishing its membership by adopting the Credentials Committee report;

2) deciding upon its rules (to the extent these will differ from those in the parliamentary authority) by adopting the report of the Committee on Standing Rules; and

3) scheduling the order in which it will consider its business by adopting the Program Committee report. [RONR (11th ed.), pp. 609–10.]

F. ESTABLISHING THE VOTING MEMBERSHIP OF THE CONVENTION

Which came first, the chicken or the egg? A convention must deal with a similar question. Before it can proceed to other business, its voting membership must be officially established. Normally, the existing membership of a group votes to admit or approve new members. Yet who can vote to certify members—approve the list of delegates—before there are any approved delegates?

The solution developed by parliamentary law is to have a Credentials Committee, whose membership is determined in accordance with the organization's bylaws, preliminarily certify a list of delegates and alternates. Those on the Credentials Committee list are provisionally seated. After the convention has been called to order, the Credentials Committee submits the list of delegates it has approved to those same delegates to be voted on. Before adopting the Credentials Committee report, which approves the list of delegates and establishes the official voting membership of the convention, the delegates tentatively seated may vote to amend the report by inserting, striking, or substituting names.

Both amendment and final adoption of the Credentials Committee report require a majority vote. Subsequently, the Credentials Committee makes supplementary reports, reflecting new registrations—normally at the beginning of each day and whenever called upon to do so by the convention, such as immediately before an important vote. Each is subject to amendment under the same process as with the initial report. Although each supplementary report replaces the roll previously adopted, it requires only a majority vote to adopt. [RONR (11th ed.), pp. 615–17.]

The convention's quorum should be set by the bylaws or by the convention standing rules. Otherwise, it is a majority of the number of delegates who actually register, regardless of whether some may have departed. [RONR (11th ed.), p. 617, ll. 29–33.]

G. CREDENTIALS CONTESTS

In the majority of conventions, the list of delegates is noncontroversial, and the Credentials Committee report is routinely adopted without debate or amendment. If you are a delegate or alternate to such a convention, you may safely skip this section.

In some conventions, however, chiefly those of political organizations, the credentials of some delegates or of entire delegations may be hotly contested. If you are a delegate or alternate to this type of convention, it is important for you to know the procedure for dealing with credentials contests, since *who* are ultimately seated as delegates will likely have great influence on *what* the convention ultimately decides when it conducts elections and formulates policies.

It is possible for there to be a dispute over the number of delegates to which a particular unit is entitled. In other cases there may be disagreement over which individuals were validly selected to represent a unit. There may even be a contest between rival groups, each claiming to be the organization's authorized unit for a given locality or subdivision.

If the Credentials Committee has serious doubt about who is entitled to be seated in any of these cases, it omits the contestants from the roll it submits (but describes the dispute in its report). On the other hand, if the committee finds the claim of one side to be legitimate, it includes that side's delegates in the list. All those listed by the Credentials Committee as delegates are provisionally seated as voting members of the convention, pending the convention's action on the Credentials Committee report.

At the beginning of the first business meeting, following any opening ceremonies, the report of the Credentials Committee is given by its chairman. The chairman concludes by moving that the roll of delegates submitted with the report be the official roll of the voting members of the convention.

At this point, any delegate who has been included on the list may move to amend the report, for example:

a) **"by striking out** 'Ingrid Nolan' **in the roll of delegates as submitted, for** the state of Missouri,"
b) **"by adding, 'provided that the name of** Luis Garcia **be added to the roll of delegates, as submitted, as a delegate from** the state of Missouri,'" or
c) **"by striking out** 'Ingrid Nolan' **and insertin**g 'Luis Garcia' **in the roll of delegates as submitted, for** the state of Missouri."

No single amendment may apply to more than:

1) a single challenged delegate; or
2) a single delegation, all of whose members are challenged on the same grounds.

None of those involved in the case may vote on the amendment. However, those seated by the Credentials Committee, even if contested in a case not yet reached, can vote on all cases except their own. If any such amendment is adopted, anyone seated by the amendment can thereafter vote on further motions connected with the consideration of the report, while those unseated by it can no longer vote and must leave the delegate (or alternate) section of the hall. [RONR (11th ed.), pp. 615–16.]

H. ADOPTION OF THE
CONVENTION RULES

A convention is of course governed by the rules in the organization's bylaws and its adopted parliamentary authority. However, it almost always is advisable to adopt rules specifically for the convention, which contain additional provisions, and which in some cases vary from those in the parliamentary authority. For example, the limited time and press of business at a convention usually require strict limits on the time a delegate may have for debate.

The Standing Rules of the Convention normally include two types of rules. Some (for example, limiting speakers to two minutes) are in the nature of special rules of order; see page 86. Others (for example, requiring delegates to wear badges) are administrative standing rules; see page 87.

Before the convention, a Committee on Standing Rules, whose members are selected in accordance with provisions in the organization's bylaws, drafts the proposed rules. The rules it proposes are handed to each delegate and alternate upon registration.

Immediately following adoption of the initial Credentials Committee report, the convention considers the report of the Committee on Standing Rules. Normally the committee chairman reads the proposed rules in their entirety. He or she concludes by moving their adoption, on behalf of the committee.

The proposed rules may then be debated and amended. Any delegate may demand a separate vote on any individual rule, in which case the convention votes first on all of the rules not separated out by such demands, together, and then proceeds to consider each of the rules thus separated.

To adopt any individual rule thus separated or any new rule sought to be added, a two-thirds vote is required if it is in the nature of a special rule of order. If it is an administrative standing rule, only a majority vote is required to adopt it. A vote on the package of rules, including some of each nature, requires a two-thirds vote to adopt.

Once the rules have been adopted, they may be suspended for a particular purpose by a *majority* vote, in which case the relevant rule in the parliamentary authority becomes applicable. To suspend a rule in the parliamentary authority (alone or in combination with convention standing rules) requires a two-thirds vote.

To amend or rescind a standing rule of a convention once adopted requires a two-thirds vote of the delegates present and voting or a majority vote of all the delegates who have registered, unless it is an administrative standing rule, in which case it can also be rescinded or amended by a majority vote of the delegates present and voting after notice on at least the preceding day. [RONR (11th ed.), pp. 618–24.]

I. ADOPTION OF THE CONVENTION PROGRAM

The final step in "organizing" a convention is also a very important one. It is the adoption of the convention program, which includes the agenda for the business meetings plus the schedule of special events—forums, workshops, banquets, etc. Unless the rules are suspended, only those items that are on the agenda may be considered by the convention, and they will be dealt with in the order and at the times they are listed. Frequently, the agenda will set a limited time for the consideration of some or all items.

Because items not listed will not be considered, and items toward the end of the agenda have a greater chance of never being reached if there are delays, you should pay close attention to the proposed agenda, and be prepared to propose amendments to it if needed to ensure that your policy objectives and those of your unit are given adequate consideration.

A Program Committee, whose members are selected in accordance with procedures in the bylaws, prepares a proposed program before the convention begins. This proposed program is provided to each delegate upon registration and is followed as a guide until the time for its formal adoption. This comes immediately after the convention adopts its standing rules. The committee chairman reports on behalf of the Program Committee and concludes by moving the adoption of the program as printed (or perhaps with corrections or changes which he or she announces).

The proposed program is then debatable and amendable. Both amendment and final adoption require a majority vote.

Once adopted, the agenda can be changed only by a vote of two thirds of those present and voting or by a vote of a majority of all the delegates registered, or—as is frequently done—by unanimous consent. [RONR (11th ed.), pp. 629–30.]

J. CONSIDERATION OF RESOLUTIONS

Apart from the conduct of elections and the reception of reports, the bulk of the time at business meetings of your convention is likely to be taken up in consideration of resolutions. Commonly a rule of the convention requires either that proposed resolutions be submitted directly to a Resolutions Committee, sometimes a specified time in advance of the convention, or that immediately upon their introduction on the floor of the convention resolutions be automatically referred to that committee.

The authority of the Resolutions Committee varies depending on the rules of each organization or convention. It ranges from merely having power to put proposed resolutions into proper form and to organize them in the order in which they are to come before the convention, to having power to decide which resolutions will or will not come before the convention (typically subject to the authority of the convention to overrule the committee). An intermediate level of authority requires the committee to report all resolutions properly submitted to it, but allows it to make recommendations for or against passage, or for amendments. Like the other convention committees previously discussed, its membership is selected in accordance with procedures in the organization's bylaws.

Ordinarily the Resolutions Committee holds hearings on the resolutions submitted to it, and then meets in executive session (privately) to review them and prepare its report. [RONR (11th ed.), pp. 637–38.]

Sometimes the Resolutions Committee itself originates resolutions. Commonly, these include one or more "courtesy resolutions" recognizing those who have contributed to the convention. In some organizations, the Resolutions Committee prepares a detailed "platform" designed to express the group's views.

Except for resolutions that originate in the Resolutions Committee, those on which it reports are treated as if they have already been moved and seconded. During the committee's report, its chairman does move adoption of amendments it is proposing, as well as the adoption of resolutions that originate with it.

The resolutions on which the Resolution Committee reports to the convention are debated, amended, and voted on as in the case of motions reported to an assembly by any committee. [See pp. 164–65; RONR (11th ed.), pp. 633–40.]

INDEX

Page numbers for definitions are in **boldface**.

TABLES

CONTENTS

TABLE A:

HANDLING MOTIONS
AS CHAIR

Stating the Motion

CHAIR:	It is moved and seconded that . . . [repeating motion]

Putting the Motion to a Vote

When no one seeks the floor to debate	Are you ready for the question? (or **Is there any further debate?**) [If no one then seeks the floor, proceed to take the vote.*]
Voice Vote	
VOTING BY VOICE [Stand]	**The question is on the adoption of the motion that** [repeat or clearly identify the motion]. **Those in favor of the motion, say** *aye*. [PAUSE] **Those opposed, say** *no*. [PAUSE] **The ayes have it and the motion is adopted.** OR **The noes have it and the motion is lost.**

---

*If no further debate or amendment is in order, proceed to take the vote WITHOUT asking either of these questions. If amendment but not debate is in order, ask either "Are you ready for the question?" or "Are there any [further] amendments?"

TABLE A

Other Methods of Voting

Rising Vote	
CHAIR: [Stand]	The question is on the adoption of the motion that [repeat or clearly identify the motion]. **Those in favor of the motion will rise.** [PAUSE] **Be seated. Those opposed will rise.** [PAUSE] **Be seated.**
If majority vote	The affirmative has it and the motion is adopted. OR The negative has it and the motion is lost.
OR, if 2/3 vote	There are two thirds in the affirmative and the motion is adopted. OR There are less than two thirds in the affirmative and the motion is lost.
Counted Rising Vote	
CHAIR: [Stand]	The question is on the adoption of the motion that [repeat or clearly identify the motion]. **Those in favor of the motion will rise and remain standing until counted.** [PAUSE] **Be seated. Those opposed will rise and remain standing until counted.** [PAUSE] **Be seated. There are ___ in the affirmative and ___ in the negative.**
If majority vote	The affirmative has it and the motion is adopted. OR The negative has it and the motion is lost.
OR, if 2/3 vote	There are two thirds in the affirmative and the motion is adopted. OR There are less than two thirds in the affirmative and the motion is lost.

Show of Hands Vote	
CHAIR: [Stand]	The question is on the adoption of the motion that [repeat or clearly identify the motion]. Those in favor of the motion will raise the right hand. [PAUSE] Lower hands. Those opposed will raise the right hand. [PAUSE] Lower hands.
If majority vote	The affirmative has it and the motion is adopted. OR The negative has it and the motion is lost.
OR, if 2/3 vote	There are two thirds in the affirmative and the motion is adopted. OR There are less than two thirds in the affirmative and the motion is lost.
Counted Show of Hands Vote	
CHAIR: [Stand]	The question is on the adoption of the motion that [repeat or clearly identify the motion]. Those in favor of the motion will raise the right hand and keep it raised until counted. [PAUSE] Lower hands. Those opposed will raise the right hand and keep it raised until counted. [PAUSE] Lower hands. There are ___ in the affirmative and ___ in the negative.
If majority vote	The affirmative has it and the motion is adopted. OR The negative has it and the motion is lost.
OR, if 2/3 vote	There are two thirds in the affirmative and the motion is adopted. OR There are less than two thirds in the affirmative and the motion is lost.

When Chair's Vote Affects Result of Counted Vote (Rising or Show of Hands)	
CHAIR:	There are ___ in the affirmative and ___ in the negative.
If majority vote	The chair votes in the affirmative, making ___ in the affirmative and ___ in the negative, so that the affirmative has it and the motion is adopted. OR The chair votes in the negative, making ___ in the affirmative and ___ in the negative, so that the negative has it and the motion is lost.
OR, if 2/3 vote	The chair votes in the affirmative, making ___ in the affirmative and ___ in the negative, so that there are two thirds in the affirmative and the motion is adopted. OR The chair votes in the negative, making ___ in the affirmative and ___ in the negative, so that there are less than two thirds in the affirmative and the motion is lost.

Responding to Common Motions and Circumstances

Parliamentary Inquiry	MEMBER:	A parliamentary inquiry, please.
	CHAIR:	**The member will state his (her) inquiry.**
	MEMBER:	[EXAMPLE:] Is a motion to adjourn now in order?
	CHAIR:	**[Answer the question.]**
Request for Information	MEMBER:	Mr. President, I have a request for information.
	CHAIR:	**The member will state his (her) request.**

	MEMBER:	[EXAMPLE:] The motion calls for a lot of money to be spent. Will the Treasurer tell us how much money the Society has in the bank?
	CHAIR:	[Answer the question, or recognize to speak the person who can answer, e.g.:] **The Treasurer will please state the balance in the treasury.**
Point of Order	MEMBER:	Point of order!
	CHAIR:	**The member will state his (her) point of order.**
	MEMBER:	I make the point of order that . . .
	CHAIR: [Stand]	**The chair rules that the point of order is/ is not well taken.** [Explain reasons.]
Appeal	MEMBER:	I appeal from the decision of the chair. (Second.)
	CHAIR:	**The decision of the chair is appealed from.** [State clearly the exact question at issue and the reasons for your decision.] **The question is, "Shall the decision of the chair be sustained?"**
	DEBATE [Stand while debating]	[If the appeal is debatable (see Table D), members may speak only once, but you may speak twice, the second time in rebuttal at the debate's close:] **As the rules permit, the chair will speak first. . . .** [After others debate:] **The chair intends to speak in rebuttal. Are there others who wish to speak first?** [Pause; if no response, give your rebuttal.]
	PUTTING THE MOTION TO A VOTE CHAIR: [Stand]	**The question is, "Shall the decision of the chair be sustained?" Those in favor of sustaining the chair's decision, say *aye*. Those opposed to sustaining this decision, say *no*.** [Majority in *negative* required to overturn your decision.]

Responding to Common Motions and Circumstances *(continued)*

Previous Question	MEMBER:	I move the previous question. (Second.)
	CHAIR:	**It is moved and seconded to order the previous question. Ordering the previous question will cut off any further debate. Those in favor of the previous question will rise. [PAUSE] Be seated. Those opposed will rise. [PAUSE] Be seated.**
	If two thirds	**There are two thirds in the affirmative and the previous question is ordered. The question is now on the adoption of the motion** [state in full the motion on which the *Previous Question* has now been ordered, and immediately take the vote on it].
	OR, if less than two thirds	**There are less than two thirds in the affirmative and the motion for the previous question is lost. The question is now on** [state the immediately pending motion]. [Debate may now resume.]
Recess	CHAIR:	**The meeting stands recessed for 15 minutes.**
	RESUME CHAIR: [Stand]	**The meeting will come to order. The time of recess has expired. The question is on** [state pending motion].

TABLE B:

WHEN CHAIR STANDS AND SITS

CHAIR STANDS	When putting question to a vote When calling a meeting to order or declaring it adjourned When ruling on point of order (or debating appeal)
CHAIR SITS	When a member is speaking in debate
OTHERWISE CHAIR STANDS OR SITS AS HE OR SHE CHOOSES	

TABLE C:

CONDUCTING A MEETING
AS CHAIR

CALL TO ORDER	[Stand] The meeting will come to order.
OPENING CEREMONIES OR EXERCISES	The invocation will be given by . . . . The singing of the national anthem will be led by . . . . The Pledge of Allegiance will be led by . . . .
READING AND APPROVAL OF MINUTES	The Secretary will read the minutes. [Chair sits, Secretary stands.] [After minutes read:] **Are there any corrections to the minutes?** . . . **If there are no [further] corrections, the minutes are approved as read [corrected].**
OR, if minutes distributed before meeting	The minutes of the previous meeting have been distributed. **Are there any corrections to the minutes?** . . . **If there are no [further] corrections, the minutes are approved as distributed [corrected].**
REPORTS	[EXAMPLES:] May we have the Treasurer's report. The chair recognizes the chairman of the Membership Committee for a report. Does the Program Committee have a report?
UNFINISHED BUSINESS	**Under unfinished business, the first item of business is the motion relating to . . . , which was pending when the last meeting adjourned. The question is on the adoption of the motion** [stating the motion]. **The next item of business is . . . .**
NEW BUSINESS	Is there any new business? Is there any further new business?
ADJOURNMENT	Since there is no further business, [pause, stand, and resume slowly] **the meeting is adjourned.**

TABLE D:

TABLE OF RULES RELATING TO MOTIONS

A much more comprehensive version of this table is found in Table II in RONR (11th ed.), tinted pages 6–29.

Motion	Debate?	Amend?	Vote
Adjourn[1]	No	No	Majority
Amend	Yes	Yes	Majority
Amend Something Previously Adopted	Yes	Yes	(a) Maj. with notice; or (b) 2/3; or (c) maj. of entire membership[2]
Appeal	Normally[3]	No	Majority in negative required to reverse chair's decision
Commit	Yes	Yes	Majority
Debate, Close (Previous Question)	No	No	2/3
Debate, Limit or Extend Limits of	No[4]	Yes	2/3
Division of the Assembly (Demand a Rising Vote)	No	No	Demand of a single member compels a rising vote (uncounted)
Main Motion	Yes	Yes	Majority
Postpone	Yes	Yes	Majority

[1]For special circumstances in which the rules for *Adjourn* differ, see RONR (11th ed.), tinted page 6, #3 (Table II).

[2]For special circumstances in which the vote required for *Rescind/Amend Something Previously Adopted* differs, see RONR (11th ed.), page 306, line 24 to page 307, line 12.

[3]In debate on an appeal, each member may speak only once, except that the chair may speak twice, the second time at the close of debate. *Appeal* is **not** debatable if it relates to indecorum or transgression of the rules of speaking, or to the priority of business, or

Motion	Debate?	Amend?	Vote
Previous Question	No	No	2/3
Recess	No[4]	Yes	Majority
Reconsider	If motion to be reconsidered debatable	No	Majority
Rescind	Yes	Yes	(a) Maj. with notice; or (b) 2/3; or (c) maj. of entire membership[2]
Refer (Commit)	Yes	Yes	Majority
Suspend the Rules (rules of order)	No	No	2/3[5]
Suspend the Rules (standing rules or convention standing rules)	No	No	Majority[5]
Voting, motions relating to	No[4]	Yes	Majority[6]

if made while an undebatable question is immediately pending or involved in the appeal. RONR (11th ed.), pp. 257–58, #5; tinted page 10, #19 (Table II).

[4]Unless made while no other motion is pending. RONR (11th ed.), tinted p. 14, #31; tinted p. 24, #72; tinted p. 28, #85.

[5]For special circumstances in which the vote required for *Suspend the Rules* differs, see RONR (11th ed.), page 261, lines 15–17.

[6]2/3 required for motion to close the polls. RONR (11th ed.), tinted p. 29, #84.

TABLE E:

WORDS TO USE
AS A MEMBER

To Obtain Recognition and Speak

MEMBER A: [Stand]	Madam President!
CHAIR:	Mr. A.
MEMBER A:	[Say what you have to say, then sit when finished.]

To Make a Motion

After being recognized to speak:	I move that . . . .

To Second a Motion

Remaining seated, without seeking recognition:	Second!

To Make *Particular* Motions

For a more complete set of examples, see RONR (11th ed.), tinted pages 30–39 (Table III).

After Being Recognized by the Chair to Speak:	
Adjourn	I move to adjourn.
Amend	I move to amend: [EXAMPLES:] by **striking out** "blacktop" before "driveway." by **inserting** "in the meadow" after "building." by **striking out** "concrete" **and inserting** "blacktop." by **striking out** the third paragraph. by **inserting** the following paragraph on page 6 after line 5: . . . . by **substituting** for the pending motion the following: . . . .

After Being Recognized by the Chair to Speak: (continued)	
Commit or Refer	I move to refer the motion to a committee of three to be appointed by the chair.
Count Vote	I move that the vote be counted.
Debate, Close Immediately	I move the previous question.
Debate, Limit or Extend Limits of	I move that debate be limited to one speech of three minutes for each member.
Postpone to a Certain Time	I move to postpone the question to the next meeting.
Previous Question	I move the previous question.
Recess	I move to recess for five minutes.
Suspend the Rules	I move to suspend the rules and . . . .
Vote, Count	I move that the vote be counted.

Without Needing to Be Recognized by the Chair to Speak:		
Appeal [Stand]	I appeal from the decision of the chair.	
Demand a Rising Vote [Need not stand]	Division!	
Parliamentary Inquiry [Stand]	MEMBER:	A parliamentary inquiry, please.
	CHAIR:	The member will state his (her) inquiry.
	MEMBER:	[EXAMPLE:] Is a motion to adjourn now in order?
Point of Order [Stand]	MEMBER:	Point of order!
	CHAIR:	The member will state his (her) point of order.
	MEMBER:	I make the point of order that . . . .
Request for Information [Stand]	MEMBER:	Mr. President, I have a request for information.
	CHAIR:	The member will state his (her) request.
	MEMBER:	[EXAMPLE:] The motion calls for a lot of money to be spent. Will the Treasurer tell us how much money the Society has in the bank?

FOR HELP DURING A MEETING . . .

Take this book with you to meetings.

Turn back one page, and you will have handy in front of you the words you are most likely to need to use to take part in debate and make motions.

Turn back two pages for a table of the basic rules for the most common motions.

If you are chairing the meeting, keep the book open in front of you to page 193, Conducting a Meeting as Chair, but turn back to pages 187–92 for the words you need to use in handling motions and conducting votes.